JAMES C. SCHAAP

100% CHANCE OF FROGS

DEVOTIONS ▾ FOR

TODAY

CRC Publications

Grand Rapids, Michigan

Text illustrations: Paul Stoub

Copyright © 1992 by CRC Publications, 2850 Kalamazoo SE, Grand Rapids, Michigan 49560

 Printed in the United States of America on recycled paper. ⊛

Library of Congress Cataloging-in-Publication Data
Schaap, James C., 1948-
          100% chance of frogs / James C. Schaap.
              p.   cm. -- (Devotions for today)
          ISBN 1-56212-025-5 : $6.25
          1. Bible. O.T. Exodus I-XV—Meditations. 2. Teenagers—Prayer-books and devotions—English. I. Title. II. Series.
BS1245.4.S33   1992
242'.5—dc20   92-24941
          CIP
          AC

ISBN 1-56212-025-5

9 8 7 6 5 4 3 2 1

CONTENTS

PREFACE

The book of Exodus tells the tale of Israel's salvation. It relates the grand and glorious story of how God reached down into the land of Egypt and, through his servant Moses, pressured ruthless and proud Pharaoh into freeing a mob of helpless slaves. "Let my people go," God demanded, and Pharaoh finally and reluctantly did precisely that.

It is also the story of some very real people: Moses and his parents; his sister, Miriam, and his wife, Zipporah; his people, the Jews, and his great enemy, the Pharaoh. These people were frightened and brave, rebellious and obedient, wavering and firm, doubting and believing— just as we are today. Read of them and you know—these are no invention of anyone's imagination.

In the fifty-two brief meditations of this book, James Schaap brings these people and their story into your own age and into your own home. Retelling the stories and relating them to incidents in our modern life, he makes these people come alive. You will feel the stubborn trust of Puah and Shiphrah as they defy Pharaoh's order to kill the babies, see shy Zipporah meeting Moses at the village well, and hear Miriam telling her story. And all these people will speak to your own faith, calling you to trust in the amazing God who liberated this captive people.

James C. Schaap, author of 100% Chance of Frogs, is a professor of English at Dordt College in Sioux Center, Iowa. He has written many short stories that reflect on human life from a strong faith perspective. Besides his popular book of devotionals for teenagers, *Intermission,* Schaap has written three other booklets in this Devotions for Today series: *Someone's Singing, Lord; No Kidding, God;* and *Take it from a Wise Guy.*

This present book is offered with the prayer that you may read it not only for your personal enjoyment but also for your spiritual profit.

Harvey A. Smit
Editor in Chief
Education Department
CRC Publications

AN EXPLOSION OF BLESSING

....

Read Exodus 1:1-7

If we asked a dozen shoppers in some mall to draw a picture of a typical 1960s person, most would sketch a long-haired girl in torn jeans sitting cross-legged in the grass of some park. She'd be wearing a headband and a T-shirt with a peace symbol, and chances are she'd be strumming a guitar.

It's a little more difficult to imagine how our shopping-center sampling would picture the 1980s look. But the person they sketch might well be driving a convertible BMW, top down. His slicked-back hair would gleam like a magazine ad, and you'd seldom see him without his Ray-Ban sunglasses. Likely as not, Calvin Klein would have designed his faded jeans, and his Corinthian leather briefcase would be a Gucci.

As everyone knows, the word that describes this eighties prototype is YUPPIE—*Young Urban Professional.* In the States, at least, no one better personified the era than the guy who thought he had it all.

When Yuppies married, they were called DINKS—*Double Income, No Kids.* Now I understand that a number of you may think of yourselves as blessings from God, but DINKS understood very well that kids don't pay. In fact, kids cost—a lot.

There's clothes, after all—not to mention McNuggets. There are Walkmans and VCRs and Air Jordans and extension phones. In addition, at least in this house, there's Christian school tuition. My goodness, do kids cost!

Kids take time too: there are ball games, piano recitals, school programs, and teacher conferences to attend. There are clothes to wash and food to prepare and baths to give. Endless hours of energy go into raising a child—enough to tax the dickens out of your patience.

The fact is, without kids there's a whole lot more opportunity for Caribbean cruises, tennis lessons, and weekends in Las Vegas. Besides, dirty diapers smell awful. The DINKS of the eighties understood that.

Obviously, God's people, the Hebrews, were not DINKS, because the Bible tells us that the Egypt of 1500 B.C. was literally full of Jews. In fact, the whole problem with Pharaoh would never have arisen if it weren't for the fact that the Israelite population virtually exploded. Boom! Israelites everywhere.

The real point of the opening passage, however, is that kids are blessings. These many, many Jewish children were a sign that the Lord's blessing stayed with the people, even though they weren't in their home territory, even though they pitched their tents in Egypt, and even though kids, then as now, cost a bundle.

Kids cost, but they're blessings. They're gifts, after all—gifts of life.

....

We don't understand why you've chosen certain people to be your own, Lord. We probably never will. But we thank you for allowing us to be a part of your family, and for giving us love.
In Jesus' name, Amen.

POMP AND CIRCUMSTANCE

....

Read Exodus 1:8-14

People who study the Bible sometimes disagree about which historical Pharaoh was running the show when the Israelites started getting out of hand in Egypt. Some think it was Thutmose III and his son Amunhotep II, but others claim it was Seti I and his son Rameses II who acted as chairmen of the board.

We'll leave such squabbles to scholars.

Whoever the man was, picture the scene this way: Egypt is *hot*. Pharaoh's got a dozen palm wavers on the steps in front of him, fanning him down, but beneath that white headgear he's sweating anyway.

Three top musicians toot away on recorders—something from the "Top 40." Women—real beauties I imagine—sit around like knick-knacks, their long white gowns spread beneath them as they munch on bananas, brazil nuts, and pomegranates.

The court is full of notable Egyptians: Lutus, the nerd who knew all the multiplication tables by the age of four; Tutenkham, the guy who invented the mummy body wrap; and Rebilius, the bowling champion.

Now I'm pulling your leg, of course. I don't know as much about old Egyptian culture as I should. If I did, I suppose I could paint a pretty accurate picture of what Pharaoh's court looked like at this time.

I've deliberately described it as some kangaroo court because, in a cosmic sense, what happens in the passage we've read today—even though it's sad and tragic for the Israelites—seems almost silly. *Cosmic* is a word we should all use more often, I think, even though when we use it, we risk sounding like philosophers. According to my dictionary, *cosmic* means "of or belonging to the universe considered as an ordered system or totality; relating to the sum or universal system of things." Isn't that a mouthful?

Let's make it simpler. When I say that in a "cosmic" sense what happens in Pharaoh's court is silly, I mean that when we look at it from our vantage point, thousands of years later, and think of it in the context of God's bigger plans, we're able to see what happened in

Egypt in a whole different light than the Israelites could. From our point of view all these Egyptian honchos thinking that they're making world-altering decisions seems really hokey.

Pharaoh (whichever one he is) gathers Rufus, Dufus, and Slewfus, and pulls them into executive session. "Let's make hay with these Israelites," he tells them, one hand up over his mouth. "We've got to be smart, see—we've got to deal with these dorks, because they breed like bunnies, and soon enough we'll be overrun."

Rufus scratches his head. Dufus nods. Slewfus has his eye on one of the princesses.

"We'll work them to death," almighty Pharaoh says. "We'll make them build our theme parks and forget the minimum wage."

His boys all grin, toothfully . . .

Let's be clear about this. The plans Pharaoh made hurt the Jewish people. Slavery is no joke. Jewish people *died* in forced labor. But in the long view of history, those Pharaohs didn't have a chance. The world they thought they were running had—and still has—a whole different Director.

God was running the show. Way back then, like today, God was the Chief Executive Officer.

....

Lord, sometimes our best ideas seem so silly. We make plans, forgetting that you are at the controls. Help us to rely on you, for we have power only in your name. Amen.

CIVIL DISOBEDIENCE

....

Read Exodus 1:15-22

You've got to love those midwives.

High-and-mighty Pharaoh summoned two lowly midwives into his court one day because he had an idea for handling the Jewish problem.

Puah and Shiphrah were not the Surgeon Generals of Egypt. They were only midwives—Jewish women who helped mothers give birth to Jewish children. They didn't belong to any big union—my guess is that, as a lobbying group, they didn't have a nickel's worth of clout—and on top of everything else, they were only women in what was obviously a man's world.

They had to be scared stiff.

"Girls," big-time Pharaoh probably said, "watch the births closely, and if it's a boy, get rid of him."

All of this happened years ago, but I think if you hold the Bible close to your ear at this passage, even today you can hear Puah and Shiphrah gulp. They brought life into the world. And now the high-and-mighty was commanding them to bring *death* instead—to kill babies.

I'm sure midwives were not among society's rich and famous, but they did have—and they still have today—great jobs. What on earth is more exciting than birth—than new life emerging? Imagine that imbecile Pharaoh asking them to kill!

You can't help but love those midwives. They walked out of the palace, they looked at each other, and my bet is, they laughed. "The man," they said, "is bonkers. Life-bringers don't kill." Puah and Shiphrah feared God, the Bible says, and they simply disobeyed the big Egyptian enchilada. The Bible doesn't say whether they agonized over their decision for weeks and weeks. They probably didn't. They knew right away that they couldn't kill babies. So they didn't.

They didn't use a magic marker on a big piece of tagboard and protest at the office. They didn't write their congressmen or petition Pharaoh with a thousand Jewish signatures. They simply didn't obey him. And, of course, they risked their lives. Puah and Shiphrah are maybe the first biblical characters to engage in civil disobedience.

Soon Pharaoh heard that his great plan wasn't working, so he summoned them once again. He asked them why his plan wasn't working, and they lied.

"The problem is," one of them told him, "these Jewish women have their kids so fast that we don't even get there on time. They're an athletic bunch. They're in great shape, Oh great high-and-mighty."

Poor Pharaoh had to abandon Plan A. The midwives, trusting God and knowing what was right, stuck that murderous plan in Pharaoh's ear.

One more thing: midwives must have been women who didn't have children of their own. Moses, who likely wrote most of the book of Exodus, stuck in a footnote here. Because they refused to obey Pharaoh's sinful command, the midwives were blessed with families of their own.

We can remember it this way: the King of Heaven and Earth blessed their disobedience of the great high-and-mighty. Puah and Shiphrah, simply and courageously, did the right thing. And the Lord said, "Bless their hearts."

....

Lord, when things get out of hand and the only way to be a Christian is the way that leads to criticism, help us to be strong, like the midwives. Help us to always do what's right. Lead us with your hand. Amen.

HUSH, LITTLE BABY

....

Read Exodus 2:1-2

The Levite man lay motionless, awake on his bed of straw. Beside him, his wife was awake also, her body stiff and rigid, as if at attention. He didn't have to see her eyes to know she was awake. After ten years together, you know, he thought. You don't need to talk about your fear when it lives in you so deeply.

The sounds their new boy-child made rustling in his bed of straw echoed off the walls, every turn a startling announcement in the night's silence. She'd fed him four times since she'd put him to sleep—whenever they'd heard the first whispers of his uneasiness. She'd fed him again and again because they couldn't let the baby cry. Certainly not at night. Not a whisper. Pharaoh himself had ruled. How many babies had already been murdered?

It was late now, or early maybe, he thought. And every child must learn to cry himself to sleep, every parent must learn to listen and not move. Too long already this had gone on, too many sleepless nights.

The baby rustled again, whimpering slightly.

The Levite man held his wife back. She should wait, he thought. She should wait until the last possible moment, or else she'd be up all night again—like last night and the night before.

He remembered how he'd waited when the midwives helped her deliver, how he'd stood in the street, just outside the door. The look on the midwife's face had told him everything. He knew it was a boy-child, and every Jew knew a boy meant death. Even so, the midwife smiled bravely. "Come in," she said. "He's so strong."

The baby had lain beside his mother, strong and silent then. He was only hours old, but he had the look of someone who would be important in God's plan—perfect arms and legs, a vitality unusual in a newborn . . .

The man's thoughts were interrupted by a cry. The baby was getting restless, but the Levite man still held his wife back. She had to let the boy alone. These endless nights of sleeplessness couldn't go on.

"But we can't—" she said. He covered her lips lightly with his fingers.

Their other two children slept innocently beside them.

They waited together in the dark, but the baby didn't settle down. He started crying louder, and the Levite woman finally broke from her husband's grasp. She went to the baby quickly to try to silence him.

The Levite man looked out the window to empty, shadowed streets where the glow of morning slowly opened over the huts across the way. He could hear the child fussing at his mother's breast—as if he hadn't drunk less than an hour ago, as if he hadn't been up nearly all night long.

The Levite man held his hands up to his face. He lay on his back in the darkness and covered his eyes because he knew they couldn't keep the boy-child any longer. There was no room for this perfect baby.

The boy-child, he knew, had to go. He knew that his wife, standing there nursing her child, understood what had to be done, too, but that didn't make it any easier. He tried to think of something in life that could be worse than having to lose this boy, something . . .

Already the morning was coming, but to him everything was darkness.

....

In the darkest moments of our lives, be with us. In those times when the skies themselves seem to fall, give us the touch of your hand to keep us safe.
Amen.

COMING HOME

....

Read Exodus 2:3-7

There is so much you don't know about a woman when you marry her. When I asked my wife to marry me, I knew I loved her. But I had no idea how special she was. I had no way of knowing about the faith that lives so richly in her.

I soon learned. Living with my wife day by day made me aware that she had eyes of faith that helped her see beyond our village, beyond our slavery, beyond the here and now. That's why I believe she knew what would happen when she put our precious boy-child in the reed basket she'd made so lovingly. I think somehow she knew. I don't know how, because I don't know everything there is to know about her. But I believe she knew.

It was all her plan, of course. Once we'd agreed that it had to be done, that we were risking the lives of the rest of the family, that we couldn't keep our precious boy-child, she started preparing. Every night, just before dark, she'd quietly weave the reeds she'd picked herself from the river bank. She'd smooth on the pitch, as if with her hands she could create a basket so perfect that it could keep this baby—our boy-child—alive.

It was her idea to send our daughter Miriam to the river too. She told me that a child, a ten-year-old, would seem innocent. She said Miriam, whose eyes are nearly as large and loving as her mother's, would be much less suspicious-looking than a nursing mother.

But when my wife came back to the house that morning after leaving Miriam and the baby at the river, she was crying. I think she had all the faith in the world that our boy-child would not fall to Pharaoh's terrible law, but when she returned, she stood before me and cried just the same.

"Now it's up to the Lord," she told me. She looked into my eyes, and I could see all the pain and horror of the past few hours reflected in her face. I took her into my arms, and we cried together.

That's where we were standing, both of us together, when little Miriam came back home carrying the boy-child, her face swimming in tears. She had our baby her arms, in the very blankets my wife had wrapped him in.

"Moses," Miriam said. "She told me his name is Moses."

My wife took the baby from her and carried him to the street to nurse him. To the *street*! She sat outside in the sun with our own baby, showing him to the world.

I think she knew all along it would end this way. My wife has more faith than I know.

....

Give us the faith of so many people of long ago, Lord. Empower us with faith that can move mountains. Don't let us give up. Give us strength that can carry us over the toughest moments we'll ever face. In Jesus' name, Amen.

MIRIAM'S STORY I

....

Read Exodus 2:3-10

The story I want to tell you starts a long time ago, back in the days when my little brother was born. It starts in those days when I watched my mother use pitch to line a basket she'd made. Days before, I'd seen her braid the reeds slowly into a little tub, her fingers moving quickly.

When the baby was first born, I had been eager for my parents to name him. "What is the baby's name?" I had asked my father once.

"Well, Miriam," he said, "for a while at least he will have no name." He smiled then, as if to apologize, and brushed the hair out of my eyes.

"Why?" I said.

He put his hands on my shoulders. "Never speak of the baby, Miriam," he told me. "Play with him and hold him—we want you to care for him. But promise you will never speak of him."

I promised. Although he didn't explain, I understood. My father had never told me of the law about boy-children, but I knew. I was old enough to understand. None of my friends, not one, had a baby brother. There *were* no baby brothers.

So we never talked of our boy-child, inside or outside the house—not until the morning mother had finished the little reed basket. "Miriam," she said. She pointed to the place beside her and asked me to sit. "I am going to put him in the Nile," she said. "I am going to float this basket at the place where the Princess bathes. Do you understand?"

I nodded because I dared not speak.

"I want you to stay there," she said. "I want you to watch closely to see what happens, and use your head, Miriam. Think."

Then she said it, for the first time. "This child is your brother, Miriam," she told me, "and the Lord has a plan for him."

I didn't ask her how she knew such things because whenever I held him and rocked him, I knew it too.

I don't think my mother knew for certain that the princess would take our baby out of the water. But maybe she did. Mother cried when she left the river bank, but her lips were firm as she looked at me and pointed to the spot where I should hide.

Just imagine how I felt when the princess herself stepped into the reeds, and the baby started crying like he did at night! As I watched, the princess drew the baby out of the basket, held him up away from her, and saw what we saw—that this baby boy was something marvelous. She knew it too. I know she did.

So I didn't have to think. I ran to the riverside, eager to finally talk to someone about my baby brother. "I know a woman," I said, "a Hebrew, who will nurse the baby."

She stooped to show me the baby. "I will name him Moses," she said, "because I drew him from the water." Then she put him in my arms.

"Moses," I sang to him. "Moses, Moses, Moses"—all the way home.

....

Lord, we thank you for this story of your love.
Help us to remember it. Help us never to
forget your love. Amen.

EDUCATION WITH A DIFFERENCE

....

Read Exodus 2:11-15

This passage of Exodus is really depressing for me as a teacher. You see, once Moses was old enough for school, the princess probably enrolled him at the nearest Egyptian educational institution for royalty. Let's call it SPAMM, the School for Pharaohs And other Muck-a-Mucks.

Moses was probably given the best Egyptian education he could get. SPAMM, after all, was once considered the Harvard of the Nile. Not a snap course in the curriculum. Being a student there meant heavy studying and the privilege of being exposed to the best ideas of Egyptian culture—art, literature, language, philosophy, science. A SPAMM diploma was likely nothing to sneeze at.

But here's the depressing part: the very best Egyptian education finally didn't mean diddly. Once he graduated, Moses was walking along the street, whistling something from some Egyptian musical, when he saw a fight. And it wasn't at all a fair fight, because the Egyptian guy had a whip. Moses, the Jew with a really splendiferous Egyptian education, never batted an eye. He went in, dukes high, forgetting everything he had ever learned about high ideas, and he shut out the Egyptian's lights.

The world's best education, it seems, couldn't shake Moses's personal feelings about his people. According to Acts 7, Moses wasn't just some hair-trigger kid spoiling for a fight either. He was already forty years old. He was a privileged person—royalty. But at that moment, he was also a sneaking, low-down murderer.

Don't get me wrong. I like the fact that he supported the underdog, and there's a lot of comfort in the knowledge that throughout all that education, Moses didn't forget who he was.

But I'm a teacher of ideas, of literature—a Christian teacher. I like to think that what I teach makes a difference—that it changes students, develops them, molds them into something. Otherwise, why teach literature? Why not just teach people how to fix shoes or hair or teeth or rubber tires? Who cares about ideas?

All that Egyptian education didn't make Moses an Egyptian. And yet it must have done some good. After all, it was part of God's plan. God himself sent Moses to SPAMM, knowing it was the best school around. God knew that later on, when Moses had to deal with these Egyptians under some pretty tense circumstances, his excellent education would come in handy.

But no matter how much time he spent in school, murdering the Egyptian proves Moses still had a lot to learn. He may have known the world's great books, but he acted like a criminal. His loyalties were right—they were with God's people. But he murdered a man without even considering whether it was right or wrong.

Moses may have been a graduate of SPAMM, but the Lord God of Israel had a few lessons to teach him before this man would be ready to lead the Israelite people. Moses still had lots and lots to learn.

Maybe the greatest lesson that the most educated of believers has to learn, even today, is to wait on God's time. Moses jumped right in without thinking, just assuming he was righteous. He had more to learn all right—out in the desert, miles away, at a school that ran on God's time.

....

Dear God, give us patience. When we want
something, we want it now. Teach us that your time
is our best time; teach us how to live as if you are in
charge. Merciful Father, forgive our impatience.
Amen.

STRANGER IN A STRANGE LAND

....

Read Exodus 2:14-21

We were seated in a fine restaurant just outside of Arnhem, the Netherlands, my family and I, just about to order dinner from a menu we couldn't begin to understand. And we were very, very uncomfortable.

In the Netherlands people don't eat at restaurants as often as they do in North America, so there are fewer of them. What's worse, there are really no *family* places at all: no Sambos, no Country Kitchens, no Ponderosas, no Perkins. You can get yourself a Big Mac, but only in the very center of big cities. Besides, who goes to Europe for Big Macs?

So come dinner (not lunch), you've got only two choices—really big and fancy places or french fries and mayonnaise in some greasy spoon. That night, we'd chosen "big and fancy."

In the Netherlands, of course, the menus are written in Dutch. If you don't know Dutch and you want to know what you're ordering, you have to ask about every last item.

The place we chose was jumping, full of rich people—we could tell by the half glasses hung on gold chains around their necks. And there we were, four hungry foreigners in rumpled sweat clothes who didn't have a clue about what we were about to order—except that it was going to cost us fifteen bucks a plate!

Our waitress was terribly busy. She rolled her eyes when we had to ask about *kip* and *zoep*. So we ordered quickly to avoid embarrassment. Something cheap. Anything. Right then we would have given a whole garden of tulips for one measly quarter pounder, skip the cheese. Or how about a shake, for pete's sake? For one hungry moment, we all wished we were back home.

All around us, people were having a good time, raising dainty napkins to their lips as if dining were a sumptuous art that common rabble lack the brains to do well. And there we sat, all thumbs—four really ugly Americans, helpless in the middle of all that untranslatable life.

No one cared that we couldn't understand. That's the thing. No one even saw us. We were invisible. We didn't even exist. We didn't matter.

I will never understand the real problems that all immigrants face, whether they be Chinese or European or Central American. But that night I learned at least a bit of how empty it feels, how invisible, not to belong. It's as if you aren't even there.

It's easy to get depressed when no one acknowledges who you are. It's easy to be resentful. It's easy to want to go home. It's even easy to cry.

Moses must have felt something of that loneliness out in Midian. He must have felt alone, somehow, even though he had a new wife. When his first son was born, he called that boy Gershom, meaning, "I have become an alien in a foreign land."

Moses must have felt a whole world turning without him. He must have felt abandoned, a refugee and an outlaw. Here was a man who'd had the best of all Egyptian educations, who'd hung around the court, who'd been a part of Egyptian life. But in Midian, he must have felt invisible.

But the Lord hadn't lost sight of Moses. Never once was he out of God's line of vision. Loneliness was a part of God's lesson plan for Moses, the leader of the Israelites. Even when he felt invisible, God was watching closely.

....

Lord, we thank you for being with us wherever we go, north or south, east or west. We know that we are never alone because you are by our side. Thank you for always being there. Amen.

A BLOODY PROMISE

....

Read Genesis 15:8-18; Exodus 2:23-25

I didn't invent ancient Jewish rituals, so don't blame me if what I'm about to explain turns your stomach. What's more, all of this was done long before animal-rights activists started griping about how we treat lab rats and farm mink, not to mention corn-fed beef. I'm sorry to have to bring it up, but it's got to be said, so take a seat in the sidecar here, and let's go back to Genesis.

Here's the blood and guts. If the ancients wanted to make dead sure that they could trust each other, they made a covenant, a promise, a pledge, a sort of "you scratch my back and I'll scratch yours" pact, except for keeps. And they had a bloody way of doing it.

Here's a "for instance." Mario's farm sits on the edge of a forest preserve that's full of lunatic Micro Goombas. By himself, he can't handle those idiots, so he goes over to his neighbor, Luigi, for help.

Luigi is a powerhouse. He's got this mega bug spray left over from the Forty Years War, and the Micro Goombas are scared to death of him.

But Luigi has this other problem. His neighbors, the Red Koopa Troopas, occasionally emit highly offensive fumes. They stink. And he can't do a thing about it.

Mario's got a huge fan. So Mario and Luigi sit down and decide to make this promise, this covenant, with each other. "My fan," Mario says, "for your big jug of bug spray."

Luigi smiles. "Amen," he says, and he pulls out his Bic pen.

Now if these two characters were Israelites, they'd do something that seems really ugly. They'd go outside, pick out some of their best livestock, and cut them in half. That's right. Whomp! Cut them in half. Then they'd lay half a bull on one side of the driveway, and the other half on the other side. Blood everywhere.

Then the two of them—get this—would parade down the middle, almost like a married couple walking down the center aisle in church.

Why? It's gross alright, but easy to understand. What Mario and Luigi are doing when they march down the bloody center aisle is saying that they too will be cut in pieces should they fail to keep their word. It's a bloody way to sign a contract, but it gets the point across.

The idea you have to remember here is that way back in Genesis, God made a covenant with humanity. God promised to be there for Abram—not just for a couple of years but forever. And that promise was not just for Abram but for all believers—including Moses, and you and me, and all who believe in God.

Verses 17 and 18 of Genesis 15 show you those same sides of beef, just like the bull lined up on Luigi's driveway. But God's covenant is different from that of Mario and Luigi in one very important way. Abram doesn't have to offer God anything. There's a promise made here, God's promise, but the only one who walks between the beef chunks is (listen to this!) a smoking firepot and a blazing torch—the symbol of God Almighty. Abram doesn't even waltz through. It's all the Lord.

Why? Because God Almighty, maker of heaven and earth, doesn't need our "bug spray" or the "windmill-sized electric fan" out of our garage. The fact is, this covenant promise, like none other on earth, doesn't depend on our scratching the Lord's back. We can't anyway—no one's got that long of an arm. God does it all for us.

When God heard the groaning of the people, the Bible says, God remembered the promise. And God still does. I like that.

Thank you for being our God, Lord. Thank you for watching over us. Give us the ability to show thanks in our lives forever. In Jesus' name, Amen.

ZIPPORAH AT THE WELL

Read Exodus 2:15-22; 4:18

The day I first saw my husband is a day I shall not forget easily.

My six sisters and I were approaching the well. We are the daughters of Revel, who is also called Jethro. We have done our work at the well for as long as we can remember, so we are not afraid of going there. But on this particular day we were startled to see a stranger sitting at the very spot where we usually place our buckets.

It was early afternoon, and the desert burned in a sun that glowed white-hot against a colorless sky. He sat there alone, someone we'd never seen before. We did not speak to him. My father says that strangers at the well have no histories and are therefore dangerous.

As we worked at the well, some shepherds joined us, talking and laughing with one another. These we knew, of course. We'd seen them dozens of times at the well. Sometimes they'd say nothing. Sometimes they'd simply go about their business. But other times they'd make getting water difficult. Often they'd say things to us that we didn't dare repeat to our father, Jethro.

On that day there were four of them, men with hard features, their hair knotted and twisted by hot winds and sweat. I didn't know their names. But when they walked toward us, I knew today would be difficult. Sometimes you just know that with men. They talk and yell and laugh too loud, and you know somehow that you will be in the way.

They started talking harshly, saying bad things, and one of them, the one with a broken nose, told us to be gone. I was standing there with my hands on the rope when the one with the broken nose came over to my side and yelled, "Are you deaf?"

I wouldn't look at him.

He yanked my hands off the rope, and the pail dropped back into the well. He had hold of both my hands.

The man who would become my husband came around the other side of the well, and he said to this man, very softly, "Let her alone."

The crooked nose looked at his friends. "Who's this joker?" he said, laughing.

I hope you don't think me proud if I tell you that my husband has a beauty about him that few men have. When he stands, people become silent. I know his blood is not royal, but in his presence you feel touched immediately by a kind of power.

"These are my sisters," he said to the man with the crooked nose.

They stopped laughing, and the ugly one let go of my hands.

"Why don't you let her finish?" Moses continued.

The man who would be my husband never said a word in anger or in warning. But even though there were four of them and only one of him, the shepherds knew somehow that their games were over. They were angry that he'd humiliated them, but they left.

"And who are you?" he said, once they had withdrawn.

I could feel my sisters giggle behind me, the moment he asked.

"Zipporah," I said. "My father's name is Jethro."

The man pulled up the sleeves of his robe and took the rope in his strong hands. "May I help you, Zipporah?" he said.

Later, after we had told my father what happened, he told us to go back and get this man who had helped us, this man who now had a history.

Of all seven sisters, I was the first to the well.

....

If we praise you forever for your love and your
patience with us, we'll still never be able to repay
you for so many gifts. You have given us life, Lord.
You have taken our lives and made them sing.
Help us to better fill the world of our lives with your
song. Amen.

SUNDAY CLOTHES

....

Read Exodus 3:1-5

I was eight—or maybe nine. That Sunday morning I was up early because I had a new sports coat hanging in the vestibule closet, right next to Dad's.

Here's the way I remember it. Nobody's up. I slip into my white shirt and pull on this great new sports coat. Not bad.

But I find a hunk of cardboard sewn on a bottom edge, one of those stiff little cards with heavy stitches in all four corners. Nobody wears sewn-on tags to church.

I haul the scissors out of the drawer beneath the phone in the dining room, take the coat off, lay it on the counter, then slip the sharp blade of the scissors beneath the cardboard tag and snip.

The dumb tag doesn't come up right away—after all it's held in place by four stiff stitches. So I cut them all, and when I pick up the tag and look beneath it, the tail of my brand-new little sports coat looks like the streamers flowing from my bike handles. We're talking major slashing here. I'm in trouble up to my sternum.

First thing I do is pray for a miracle, but when I open my eyes, the rips are still there. There's no putting the Humpty Dumpty jacket back together. What I have is a new sports coat with a tail that looks like it has been thrashed through by a Toro.

My stomach drops halfway to China. There's no way out.

My parents get up, and my mother takes one look at the mess and starts whimpering, just whimpering in my dad's arms. This Sunday best has never even been worn, and already it's in shreds. Unfortunately, my mother was to sewing what the Three Stooges were to table manners.

That morning has to rank as one of the most awful moments of my life. What made it so profoundly depressing was that this butchery was carried out on Sunday clothes, my new get-up for the holiest of days.

We had a border then, a woman who lived in a spare bedroom and taught in the local school. My mother brought Mrs. Key my shredded coat, and inside of a half hour she had it looking like new—perfect, almost a miracle.

The odd thing about it was that Mrs. Key never went to church. I thought she wasn't even a Christian. Even though I was only a kid, I remember thinking how strange it was that someone who didn't go to church could do such a wonderful miracle—mending my holy clothes.

That new coat wasn't holy, of course. There's nothing sacred about Sunday outfits. In fact, there would have been nothing wrong with my going to church in that shredded coat. God wouldn't have been put out by a little frayed fabric. God doesn't demand starched collars.

And yet the first thing God says when Moses spots this miracle bush of fire is, "Take off your shoes—you're on holy ground." It's a command to show respect before none other than the Creator of Heaven and Earth. God wants Moses dressed for the occasion.

We're in the presence of God all the time, of course, not just on Sundays in church. God's address is not some burning bush in a Syrian desert. We are God's temple. God dwells in us.

And I don't think the Lord expects us to be duded up in some kind of old-fashioned Sunday best all of the time. Sweatshirts and faded jeans are just fine on many occasions.

But God is still God. He demands our respect. Notice Moses, standing there shoeless before a fiery bush that talks and never burns up.

....

No matter where we go, Lord, you are there. It's amazing to think that we can't run away—there's no mountain high enough anywhere. We are always in your presence, Lord, because you are always with us. Help us to live with that knowledge. Amen.

WHO CARES?

....

Read Exodus 3:7-10

This might sound a little naughty, but give it a try. Just for a minute put yourself in God's shoes. That's impossible, I know, but do your best. Take a quick look at history from God's perspective . . .

Once upon a time, for no apparent reason, God decides to make a world. It's great fun, of course, designing mountain ranges, pouring out oceans, and fashioning rainbow trout. Once it's finished, God sits back and says that the whole creation lacks one crowning touch, some kind of unheard-of being that's cut out of God's own mold, that's got God's image—that's right, God's own look. "I need human beings," God says.

Presto! Adam and Eve.

Their Creator fills these special beings in on everything they need to know, but once God's back is turned, the two of them go off into this luscious garden and gorge on the one tree God told them not to touch.

Now, God could have dumped us right then and there, but he didn't.

Things get worse. The world seems bound for damnation, and God gets rather perturbed about the way these creatures, created in their Maker's own image, don't give him the time of day. So God sends a flood—rain like you wouldn't believe. But he saves this one family. And do you know what? The minute Noah, the father of this family, gets off the boat, he gets drunk and humiliates himself.

There's more. Every time God lets any of us image-bearers wander off, we get lost, terribly lost—like a kid in a mall, only worse.

Here's the question: At this point, why should God care anymore? If you were God, ask yourself whether you would keep holding on to someone as stinky and insensitive as humanity. I wouldn't.

So why does God care? That's the big question.

Actually, the answer is quite simple: *Because he promised he would.*

So what? Adam and Eve broke *their* promises. So has everybody else. People break promises all the time.

But God doesn't break his promises.

Why not? Everybody else does.

Because he's God.

So what?

God created and runs every last person, place, and thing in this world—including us.

Gimme a break.

He has already!

What do you mean?

He's given us huge breaks: "I am concerned about their suffering," *God says about the people in Egypt. Read it for yourself:* "I have come down to rescue them." *Listen to the whole story.*

That's Moses and the Jews at least a million years ago.

And it's us.

Come on. What did God do for you and me?

He gave us Jesus Christ.

You mean like he gave Moses to the Israelites?

Even better.

How so?

Jesus is his very own son—the Son of God.

You're telling me Christ is part of the same promise?

Christ is the promise. Like I said, you've got to hear the whole story.

I'm listening, all right? I'm listening. Go on.

....

*None of us are capable of holding on to promises,
Lord. None of us can stick with our commitments.
You make life possible for us. You make us strong
enough to hang on—in your strength. Thank you
for promising forever to be the God of your people.*
Amen.

SEKHMET, THOUERIS, AND THE I AM

....

Read Exodus 3:11-14

It doesn't take a valedictorian to realize that we've come a long way since ancient Egypt. But sometimes it doesn't hurt to try to visualize what life was like without shopping malls and Diet Coke and Super Nintendo . . .

Imagine that you are growing up in a small town in southern Egypt—say, Edfu. (Odd name, but then so is Oostburg, where I grew up.) You are born in Edfu, you grow up in Edfu, and you'll die in Edfu. And since there are no TVs, no news networks, no magazines, no books, no telephones, and no means of traveling, all you know and ever will know is Edfu.

Maybe because you Edfuites, like people from every other small town, never get out, you create your own gods. That's what most Egyptians did. Every little burg along the Nile had its own temple to its own god—dozens of temples, in fact, for dozens of gods. Pharaoh himself was the main god, but the Egyptians had tons of second-stringers, one for just about every occasion. And these gods came and went. Some disappeared when others began inching their way up the Top 40.

What'd those gods look like? Ancient peoples tended to look in awe at nature, so their first gods looked like animals—cows, cats, lions, and hippos. Over time, those animal gods started to look part human. For instance, Sekhmet, who was part lioness and part woman, was the god who fought off epidemics; and Thoueris, part hippo and part woman, was thought to ensure fertility and a safe childbirth.

It's no wonder, then, that Moses asks the burning bush for some kind of ID. Remember, he went to school in Egypt, where every week he had a pop quiz on the current gods of lawn tennis, polo, and boccie ball. In Egypt, it would have taken an IBM to keep up with the list of gods.

"When the people ask me who this god is," Moses says, "what do I tell them?"

Then comes the most incredible answer.

I AM.

What a name!

What it told Moses, and what it tells us, is that God is *forever*. God had a past, but it wasn't really behind him. God had a future, but it was already here. In other words, God wasn't simply in Edfu or Sakkarah in 1400 B.C., or in Oostburg or Saskatoon in the 1990s. God was and would always be everywhere—the eternally present tense.

Shopping malls and Diet Coke and Super Nintendo, like Egyptian gods, will come and go, but what God wanted people to know is that this forever God would forever be there for them. After all, the God who had heard the people groaning in Egypt was about to show great power and love.

"I AM," God told Moses. Meaning forever—in all places, in all times. "Tell them that," God said. "That's who I AM."

....

It is impossible to imagine that the same God we worship was the God Moses looked to in Egypt. You are the God that the Reformers looked to, the God of Abraham Lincoln and Charlemagne. And you are our God. You still care for your people. You love each one of us. Help us to worship you in spirit and in truth. Amen.

GOD'S CRYSTAL BALL

....

Read Exodus 3:16-22

There's something really eerie about God laying out plans the way today's passage describes. God's got things nailed down; all Moses has to do is go through the motions.

Think of it this way. You've got a great coach. Everybody loves her. She knows every kid on the volleyball team, and even though she loves winning, she's always got something good to say after a game, even to the kids who sat the bench.

The day of the first game she sets you down in the locker room. You're in street clothes because it's just after school. She's asked you and the other team members to stop by for about twenty minutes to go over some things.

"This is the way it is," says Ms. Great Coach. "Tonight, we'll play Fairview. Marcie will set like she's never set before, but Fran won't get in sync. She'll try like crazy, and we'll all be pulling for her, but she won't hit with the kind of power that we're used to. We'll lose in three games—15-11, 15-8, and 16-14."

Ms. Coach puts down the chalk, even though she hasn't written a thing on the board. You're almost embarrassed.

"Next Tuesday, it's Apollo's monsters. They'll clobber us in the first game—just as if we're not even there. Then Amber will come alive. Fran will play like an all-star, and Marcie won't miss a set. It's 15-3, Apollo, first game; 15-12, us, the second; and 15-5, us, the third. Upset city. That's the way it's going to go."

For the next fifteen minutes she maps out every match you'll play, through the tournaments, one after another, as if she's got a perfect crystal ball. She tells you who's going to be strong, who's going to be weak, and who's going to bawl at the end . . .

Sound unbelievable? That's exactly how the Lord laid out the whole story for Moses.

"Listen," God said, "get the elders together and tell them. They'll listen to you. Don't sweat it."

"Okay," Moses thought. "I'm glad *you're* confident—I'm not."

"Then tell Pharaoh my people want a three-day leave to worship God." The voice never missed a step. "Pharaoh won't let you go, though, not unless I push him around a little. So I will."

Moses must have been stunned—what a game plan!

"What's more," God said, "you'll take a whole lot more than just the clothes on your backs. I'll take good care of you." The master teacher's lesson plan is already written in stone.

Imagine what Moses must have thought when it all turned out just the way the Lord had said it would: Pharaoh said no, just as God had said he would. Pharaoh finally consented, just as God had predicted. And the people of Israel left Egypt thick with jewelry—just as God had said. Imagine what Moses must have thought of God—the one who called the shots!

You see, the purpose of the Jews' deliverance was not simply to end their slavery, as terrific as that may have been. The event also helped both God's people and the Egyptians to feel God's power and love.

Moses' lesson started the day God laid out a game plan for the Egyptians. Moses was about to witness the awesome power of the Creator.

Blessed be the name of that Lord, our Lord!

....

Dear Lord in Heaven, sometimes it seems as if you're too big for us even to comprehend. To think you actually know us, individually, is so hard to swallow. But your Word tells us that you've cared for your people for centuries. May we always thank you with our love. Amen.

GO ON—GET MOVING!

....

Read Exodus 4:1-17

Let's be honest: our best attempts at understanding what goes on in God's mind are going to fail because God is God and we aren't. Sure, we're made in God's image, but God isn't made in ours.

It's interesting sometimes, though, to think of God in human terms. And when the Bible describes God that way, as it does in this passage, it's wonderful.

Start at the beginning. Moses spots a bush burning in the desert. So what? Deserts are hot. Maybe this bush got nailed by lightning.

But wait a minute. This bush isn't *really* burning. Oh, flames are jumping from its branches, all right, but the bush doesn't disintegrate. It's like somebody sprayed lighter fluid all over it, then lit it. But only the lighter fluid burns—not what's underneath it.

While Moses is still staring at this strange sight, God tells him to take off his shoes. And when Moses does, God explains that he's seen the Jews suffering and has heard their groans. God's decided to send none other than Moses himself back to Egypt to do something about it.

"Wow," Moses says, "I'm don't know that I'm up to it."

"Who said anything about your going alone?" the Lord tells him. "I'll be right there with you."

Moses' knees are still clattering. "Suppose I do go," he says. "If I speak to the elders, who am I going to say sent me?"

"The I AM," God says, and proudly outlines the whole story, explaining, step by step, exactly what's going to happen.

Moses is still scared. "What if they tell me I'm crazy?" he says.

The Lord reaches into a bag of tricks and pulls out three stunts Moses can use. Moses throws a stick on the ground, and it turns into a cobra; Moses shoves his hand into his coat, and it comes out white with leprosy. Then the Lord tells Moses that if people still don't believe him after these first two tricks, he'll be able to turn the Nile water into blood. That'll convince 'em.

Moses' teeth are still chattering. After everything he's been through already—talking to a burning bush, having his future foretold, watching a stick turn into a cobra, seeing his hand turn white with leprosy—after all of that, Moses still stands there swallowing a lot.

"You know," he says, "I-I've never been much of a talker. You can do a whole lot better than me for this, ah, job."

Now watch what happens.

The Lord blows his cool. "Now go!" he screams in verse 12. He doesn't ask anymore; he commands. "I'll tell you what to say!" he says.

Moses still chews his bottom lip. "Good Lord," he says, "please find somebody else." Five times Moses backs up.

God, mad? You betcha. "The LORD's anger burned," the Bible says, and the voice likely came blistering from the bush and assaulted Moses' ears. "What are you afraid of?" the Lord says. "I'll be with you every last minute."

Moses nods and turns. He knows better than to back off again. The Bible doesn't tell us what God thought right at that moment, but I can about imagine him shaking his head and rolling his eyes.

You've got to kind of pity poor Moses. After all, how many of us rally at the idea of serving God in difficult times? Just the same, I like that picture of God boiling over.

"Now, go!" God orders Moses. "Stop whimpering and get at it."

We're God's children all right, and sometimes, all of us—not just Moses—act like it.

....

Give us the courage, Lord, to do what you want us to do. Strengthen us in every way, so that when you ask us to do something that seems out of the realm of our possibilities, we'll do it. Empower us with your love. Amen.

A HARD(ENED) HEART

....

Read Exodus 4:21-23

I think some wise guy ought to put up a Hall of Fame for the toughest questions of all time. Make it a regular museum, and in each room put up a diorama with wax models of famous human beings twisting each other in endless tangles of arguments.

I've got the first nomination. This one has baffled people for centuries:

Is there such a thing as freedom?

People who say no claim that every last thing we do is based on something we are or have learned. For instance, if we knew every last thing about you—what your parents are like, where you come in the family, how shy or forward you are, how much you like math—we could predict a lot about your behavior. We might even be able to pinpoint which seat you'd pick if you walked into an empty math classroom. So, these people argue, since everything we do is somehow predictable, there's no such thing as freedom.

Those who stand on the other side say that of course there is such a thing as freedom, that human beings aren't some sort of monkeys acting only out of instinct, that people often do wacky things that nobody could have predicted.

You can find this hall-of-fame question in the Bible, too. In the passage for today, for example, we read about God hardening Pharaoh's heart (v. 21). If you really think about that verse, you can't help feeling a little sorry for Pharaoh. After all, what kind of a choice did he really have if the Lord stepped in and hardened his heart? None. The Lord cranked up the hardness factor and turned old Mr. P. into a monster.

So who's at fault here? Should Pharaoh drown in the Red Sea if the Lord didn't even allow him to think about the right answer? Seems unfair to me. Why not blame God? I would if I were Pharaoh.

But before we get all teary about Mr. P., we better take a look at a few more passages that are coming up. For instance, Exodus 8:15: "But when Pharaoh saw that there was relief, *he* hardened his heart . . ."

Here, God's not to blame. Pharaoh is. Or how about Exodus 7:13: "Pharaoh's heart became hard, and he would not listen . . ." In this instance, Pharaoh's heart seems to act on its own; it gets tough as leather.

So is Pharaoh to blame for the fact that he's a wretch, or is God?

Now I don't claim to be able to answer this question once and for all time. After all, I'm nominating this whole question of freedom for the Rough Question Hall of Fame because it's a titanic problem. But, here's the way I understand it. When Jesus told Peter that Peter would deny him three times before the rooster crowed, did that mean Peter was forced into it? No. Each time people asked him if he was a buddy of this Jesus, Peter swore it off. But he *chose* to deny his Lord, as Jesus Christ knew perfectly well that he would.

We don't let Peter off because Jesus knew. Should we let Pharaoh off because God told Moses ahead of time what was going to happen?

Nope. Sorry, Mr. P. You had your choice, and you blew it.

It's the same in our lives. God knows what's going to happen, all right, but that doesn't mean we don't make the choices ourselves.

It's a tough question, but that's what I think.

....

We may never really understand how much of what we do is by our own choice, Lord—and how much is your plan for our lives. But we know this—that you have a plan, and that for those of us who are in your family, that plan includes life. Help us to share our joy. In Jesus' name, Amen.

BLOODY DEMANDS

....

Read Exodus 4:18; 24-26

I don't always understand my husband.

He returns from the desert with some strange tales. He says he's seen a bush burning, that the Lord God of the Hebrews has told him in no uncertain terms that he, Moses, God's chosen vessel, must return to Egypt and demand that Pharaoh allow the Jews to wander into the desert. That's what he says, and I believe it's true. That he saw a fire seems obvious to me from the blaze in his eyes.

But that isn't all. He throws his shepherd's crook down on the floor, and it becomes a snake. I reach for my children.

Later, my father comes over, my father who is a very wise man.

"I want to go back to Egypt," Moses says, "because I want to see if any of my people are still alive."

You explain it to me. Why does he lie to my father? Why doesn't he again turn his stick into a cobra? Why does he make up a story?

Nevertheless, my father permits him to return. And before we know it, my sons and I are on the donkey, Moses walking beside us. All of that first day, he speaks maybe seven times. His eyes are as distant as Egypt, and his soul is burning.

At night we stop at a well. He touches me, and the flame inside him has become a torch. He's burning with fever. We lie down. He pulls every shred of covering over him, even though the earth still shares its warmth with us.

I can't sleep. Moses thrashes beside me, so hard I'm afraid he will wake the children. He speaks often now, and strangely.

Suddenly he sits up. "Gershom," he says, pointing. His eyes are almost vacant, and I recognize fear, even though I've never seen it so vividly on his face before. He knows the paleness of death threatens him.

Moses points at Gershom again.

I know what he wants. It is a ritual with his people, and he's spoken of it before. He breathes heavily, as if he were running, and he points again.

Moses is my husband, and though I do not always understand him or agree with him, somehow I know that this burning will do to him what it didn't do to the bush—it will consume him, it will burn him up.

So I draw the flint knife out of the donkey's bag, and I hold it over the fire until it is warm. And then I perform the ritual. It is bloody and ugly, and my son screams. I am sickened. I cry.

I take what I've cut from my firstborn, and when I touch it to my husband's feet, I find them cool.

His fever has passed. Sweat runs like joy across his temples. He has burned inside, but he has not been consumed.

"To me," I say to him, "you are a bridegroom of blood."

My husband sleeps peacefully. I am alone, in silence, as the frantic cries of my child slowly diminish, his body bloodied. I watch the path of the moon until the first gracious glow of morning awakens my husband in a comfort that seems to me a miracle.

I don't know this God of his. I don't know this God like he does. But I have seen this God attack my husband, then save him. And I know, from that night on the desert, that this God of Moses demands obedience.

Somewhere the foreskin lies on the desert, a sacrifice.

I believe in this God's power.

....

Your word sometimes seems odd and strange, Lord.
We don't understand exactly what is meant. But we
know the story of your faithfulness. We know that
you've promised your people that you will be their
God. We are comforted by that knowledge. Thank
you for your love. Amen.

MIRIAM'S STORY II

....

Read Exodus 4:27-31

When I last saw my brother, he stood trembling before my parents, his tongue loose, jabbering about how none of what had happened was his fault. He seemed proud of standing up to the Egyptians, but afraid at the same time.

I think my father was shocked to see Moses so upset. We knew what had happened. Everyone knew about the murder. But when Moses came home, he seemed nervous—and terribly changed.

He was going to run away, he told us, to Midian, to hide out until things settled down. Pharaoh wanted to kill him, he explained, and his eyes—those bright eyes—shone with terror.

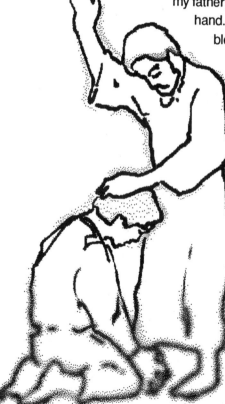

I remember watching Moses get on his knees before my father, bow to him, then reach for his hand. My father raised his right hand in a blessing.

My mother never spoke a word.

Then Moses left, backing out of the room, rubbing his hands nervously.

"It was an Egyptian," my father said once he was gone.

My mother still hadn't spoken.

"The man was mistreating one of our people," he told her. "You know the story. Everyone knows the story."

"With his hands," my mother said, her eyes vacant. "My own son killed with his hands."

That was the last time I saw my brother for many years. He was gone, lost. As long as I can remember I had been sure that the Lord had marked Moses for greatness, but when he ran away that day, all I could see was that he was a murderer.

When Moses finally returned, he had changed. He was heavier, and his shoulders seemed broader. Silver streaked the hair at his temples, and the desert sun and wind had drawn tough lines into his face. But his eyes still flashed like crystal, just as they had that morning for Pharaoh's daughter.

When Moses had knelt that day long ago and mumbled before my father, I had begun thinking of him as lost. I had thought everything I'd ever seen in him was a lie. But I had not given up on the Lord. I had prayed and worshiped God as always. I'd not forgotten the Lord, and I think deep in my heart I knew that God hadn't given up on Moses.

Still, the day Moses returned was a wonderful surprise for me. There he was, walking through the streets proudly with my brother Aaron. As they passed, people stopped whatever they were doing to watch and wonder. And as I watched him that day, it was as if something broken inside of me was suddenly made new and strong. I rejoiced to watch the man who had once been the baby I held in my arms, the baby I took from Pharaoh's own daughter. No one but the Lord himself could have saved him—I know that now, after so many years.

I'd seen our people's future in his eyes, felt God's hand in him. And then he was gone. He ran, a murderer, an outlaw who babbled and panicked like a man who has lost his way.

But he came back! The Lord brought him back to us.

Before he left for the desert, Aaron told me that God had come to him in a dream and told him to meet his brother. "Miriam," Aaron said, "can you believe it? God spoke to me! I heard his voice. He said, 'Meet your brother Moses at the mountain of God'—can you believe that?"

"Yes," I told him, smiling. "Of course I believe."

....

We praise you for your mighty works, Lord. Your Word is full of stories that prove you've never forgotten those you love. Thank you for the truth of your promises. Thank you forever. Amen.

TRULY AUDACIOUS

....

Read Exodus 5:1-5

I've got two favorite lines in the Scripture passage we read for today—one of them, I'm sure, you can guess. It belongs to the honcho, Pharaoh: "Who is the LORD?" In other words, "Who is this God?"

If you were an actor, you might have some trouble figuring out exactly how that line should be read. You could, for instance, say it in the manner of a man of ideas—inquisitively, chin in hand, eyebrows hunched, head tilted slightly—"Just who *is* this God?"

Or, you could read it like the frustrated king/god suddenly confronted by a new rival. Remember, the Egyptians had more gods than you could shake a stick at. "My word," Pharaoh might have said, "who, pray tell, is *this* God?"

But I don't think either is the right reading. My guess is you ought to read it sneeringly: "Who is this—nyuk, nyuk—God?" he says, and turns to his henchmen who all guffaw on cue.

I like the third reading because you can't help recognizing that Moses was horribly outgunned when he stepped onto Pharaoh's turf in the first place. What's more, he told Mr. P. that his people needed a three-day holiday for a festival to a God that Pharaoh didn't even know. Slaves demanding time off? It's just plain nuts.

"Come again?" Pharaoh might have said, snickering. "That this mad Hebrew comes storming the palace at all is plain crazy. But it's madness to think he can tell *me*, the mighty Pharaoh, that some unknown God demands that every last bit of Hebrew trash get a three-day pass for some desert dance." That's what Pharaoh must have thought.

"The audacity of this Jewish slave! Incredible! Pure unmitigated presumptuousness—to think he can come into the palace and make such an outrageous demand. Impudence, to think he can order a king around. It's just plain shameless."

(Those are great words, aren't they? *Presumptuous, impudent, shameless.* What they all add up to is the best one: *audacious.* Use it this way: "that incredibly audacious Moses!" I think that's exactly what Pharaoh thought.)

And that's why Pharaoh says what he does: "Who is this—nyuk, nyuk—God?"

My second favorite line from this first interview with the mighty potentate belongs to Moses. "The God of the Hebrews has met with us," he says next. "Now let us take a three-day journey into the desert to offer sacrifices to the LORD our God, or he may strike us with plagues or with the sword."

If I were Pharaoh, at that point I'd fall right off the throne. "And you think I care?" he might have said.

Moses says Pharaoh's got to give the whole bunch of slaves a weekend pass because otherwise this new God (uppercase G) will begin a reign of terror—not on Pharaoh, but on the Hebrews.

"Pardon me while I cry a million tears," Mr. P. might have said. "You think I give a rotten stick for Hebrew trash? You're nuts."

It's so utterly audacious of Moses, isn't it? So shameless, so impudent, so presumptuous.

To Pharaoh it may have seemed all of that, but to Moses what he did was plain and simple obedience. It was nothing more or less than what the Lord God Almighty had told him he had to do.

Not audacious at all. Not at all.

....

Sometimes following your Word, Lord, seems really silly. Why should we care about what you want when the whole world wants something completely different? But give us courage to fight for you. Bring us the strength to do your work in a world where your love is the greatest gift.
In Jesus' name, Amen.

BREAKING THE SPIRIT

....

Read Exodus 5:6-19

On a Saturday night, September 30, 1944, seven men who had once worked as policemen in the Netherlands waited at the Oldenaller bridge, on a country road between the towns of Putten and Nijkirk. They had gone into hiding during the Nazi occupation because they felt the enemy had to be fought, even though the battle for Holland was over.

Their orders were not to let Nazi officers pass, so when a military car came up the road to the bridge, they attacked. In the gunfight that followed, one of the attackers was wounded. One German was shot and died the next morning, Sunday. Another officer was captured. Two more soldiers, not officers, were released immediately.

The Nazis were outraged that such a thing should happen, and they reacted quickly. On Sunday morning, the entire village of Putten was surrounded by German troops. Seven people died as the soldiers entered the town. Once inside, they lined up all the people, told the women to go into the old church, and told the men to march out into the country.

A short time later the Nazi commander issued the order that the town was to be flattened, burned, incinerated. Within a few days, all the women and children were also escorted out of town, and the torch was lit. Eighty houses burned.

The commander also had the 660 Putten men transported to a prison camp at Amersfoort, the Netherlands, although for some unknown reason, sixty were freed. From Amersfoort, the men of Putten were transferred to work camps in North Germany—places, as you know, from which few men or women ever returned. In fact, only 44 of the Putten men who were transported to Germany made it out alive. An entire generation of men was destroyed by the Nazis, in retaliation for one attack on an officer's car at a lonely bridge near Putten, the Netherlands. For many years, people in Holland called Putten "the village of widows."

When they decided to burn the village of Putten and imprison all of its men, the Nazis were not interested in justice. They were interested in revenge. But more importantly, they were interested in breaking the Dutch will to resist them. They thought that if they killed an entire town, no one would ever dare to spit in their faces again.

In the same way, when Pharaoh told his henchmen to make the Hebrews find their own straw, he wasn't really interested in punishing them for being lazy. The Hebrews weren't lazy, as he said they were. That was a lie.

When Pharaoh treated the Hebrews unmercifully, he did it for the same reasons that the Nazis destroyed an entire generation of men from the village of Putten. He did it to break their wills.

The fact is, the Israelites believed that the Lord had spoken to Moses. They believed they were to go into the desert and worship the Lord. The fact is, they believed God.

That's what Pharaoh's horror was designed to eliminate—faith. It was designed to beat the tar out of the Israelites' hope.

And it worked, for a while.

But there's more to the story . . . .

....

We thank you, Lord, for not letting temptations overwhelm us, for not letting us give in when it would be so easy. Through your will, help us to keep ours strong. Give us strength to fight, day after day, for you. Amen.

PAIN

....

Read Exodus 5:20-23

Yesterday I saw this kid moseying along, taking his time moving down the sidewalk. Whatever he was doing, he was in no hurry, thinking about who-knows-what. An eight-year-old kid just poking along like thousands of other kids . . . except for one thing. He was seated in a 400-pound wheelchair. And he was making that chariot surge forward by blowing into a mouthpiece set around his cheek. A normal kid poking along, except for the wheelchair.

The kid's name is Chad, and about nine months ago he fell off a dirt pile—just fell wrong and broke some vertebrae in his neck. That why he's in a wheelchair, laid back in that huge chariot, all decked out in radio gear.

Chad loves Nintendo, plays for hours with his own special head-gear, sips and puffs the Mario Brothers through most every loony world they can get themselves into. He's also got a basketball in his room signed by every member of the Denver Nuggets.

When Chad fell off that dirt pile, more prayers were offered for him in this town than you could possibly begin to count. If prayers were hail, we'd have sent up to heaven the biggest storm ever seen in the northwest corner of the state of Iowa—thousands of prayers every week just in this corner of one little state. His relatives, wherever they live, offered hundreds more.

But yesterday Chad wasn't dribbling that Denver Nuggets basketball.

Childhood injuries, especially backbone injuries, often heal almost miraculously. Old people break a wrist, and they're out of it for months. Kids break legs, and they're trotting around in a week. So when people prayed for Chad in intensive care, they really believed that the Lord would send him home skipping.

But yesterday I saw him on the sidewalk, still in the chair.

What do we say when God doesn't answer a hundred thousand teary prayers? How can we believe God really loves us?

Moses must have asked those questions too. Can anybody really blame him for being angry? After all, he never wanted the job in the first place. He did every last thing he could to get out of it, but the Lord pushed him into a corner. "Now go," God said.

So Moses went, and now the Egyptians were furious, the Hebrews were suffering, and the Israelite foremen were ready to lynch him. Why? Because Moses didn't deliver the goods he'd promised, that's why. Why not? Because God Almighty should have left him out in Midian counting sheep.

Who can blame Moses for blowing his top at God?

But God had a plan. Let's not kid ourselves. Nearly everyone who's reading these words knows full well what happens in this story. God had a plan: the Israelite people would go free, and Pharaoh would get the shaft.

But sometimes it's pretty hard to keep the idea of God's plan in focus—both for Moses and for us. Yesterday I saw Chad on the sidewalk, and he wasn't dribbling that basketball. Doesn't God answer prayer?

Moses' story tells us God's got plans. All I can do is tell myself over and over that God's got a plan for Chad, just as he had for Moses.

God has a plan. God has a plan. God has a plan. God has a plan.

··

Lord, bless Chad, in whatever condition he is.
We thank you for sparing his life when you could
have taken it. If it be your will, heal him. Help us to
have the faith it takes to see your hand in our lives.
Amen.

GOD'S LITANIES

....

Read Exodus 6:1-13

A lot of you probably don't have the slightest idea what the word *litany* means, but almost everyone would recognize the name of the man who used a litany as part of his most famous speech. It's probably the most memorable litany used by a speaker since World War II. In fact, this litany—at least its most repeated phrase—is one of the reasons you remember the preacher who used it.

Tell you what. Let's make this a contest. I'll give you the name of the preacher, and you tell me the famous line. Okay?

The preacher's name is Dr. Martin Luther King, Jr. What's the most famous line of his most famous litany?

You've got it: the line is "I have a dream."

Chances are almost everyone who's reading this right now guessed that answer. If you didn't, you're probably kicking yourself.

A *litany*, according to my dictionary, is "a form of prayer consisting of a series of supplications to God with set responses by the congregation." But today *litany* means a little more than that. A *litany* can simply be a long list—as it was in the "I Have a Dream" speech. What Martin Luther King, Jr. did is recite a long series of dreams he had of a nation that had thrown off racism. "I have a dream," he'd say. Then again, "I have a dream that one day A-L-L of God's children . . ." You know the way it goes.

There's something wonderful about repetition. Ask any kid. Dr. Seuss knew it when he wrote about hating green eggs and ham. A litany, sometimes a series of repetitions, is a way of making a point, of really setting the idea in the mind of the hearer.

God uses a litany in response to Moses' anguish in today's Scripture passage. If you look closely, you'll find seven times in three verses that the Lord spells out plans and promises for the Israelites.

"I *will* bring you out," God says first; then, "I *will* free you from being slaves, I *will* redeem you, I *will* take you as my people, I *will* be your God, I *will* bring you to the land I swore to give to Abraham, and I *will* give it to you as a possession. Seven "I wills" right in a row. That's a litany.

And remember where Moses is—mucking around in the pits with a big fat lip, feeling sorry for himself. He'd taken God's orders to the Israelites, then to Pharaoh, just as he'd been told. But instead of freeing God's people, Pharaoh broke their backs and made them collect their own straw. Everybody was enraged, including Moses. God's litany in these verses is designed to bring home the truth once more. It's easy to picture God pounding the podium with every "I will."

But there's another, even more important litany in this passage. "I am the LORD," God says. Four times (vv. 2, 6, 7, and 8) God repeats that statement, as if to make absolutely sure that Moses knows who he's dealing with. "I AM the LORD," God says.

And don't you forget it.

....

You never leave us, Lord, but often enough we seem to leave you. Sometimes it's only because we forget you. Thank you for your promises, because without you, we would be lost forever. Amen.

WHAT'S IN A NAME?

....

Read Exodus 6:13-27

Anybody blessed with as weird a name as *Schaap* has to wonder from time to time where on earth it came from.

I've now got two theories. Here's one. This strange Dutch name was taken by a family who lived on an island in the North Sea, a place called Terschelling, a little place where some people tended sheep. When Dutch people were required to take last names (we're talking hundreds of years ago here), some yokel named Cornelius probably stood at the desk in the county courthouse, thinking about his flock back on the farm. So he said, simply, "sheep." Thus, we're named after a profession. That's not odd, really. Tons of people named Cooper are named after making kegs.

But I've got a second theory, now, an idea given to me by a man in the Netherlands, a historian who knows something about naming. He says I probably had Jewish roots way back when. He claims that when Jews were persecuted in western Europe (years ago again), many of them came to the Netherlands. Holland offered them safety on two conditions: (1) that they joined the local church; and (2) that they took Dutch names.

This historian claims that many Jewish people took very simple names, like "sheep" or "silver" or "chicken." When they stood at the county courthouse desk, they looked out the window and saw a couple of ewes. "Sheep," they said, and presto! they were Dutch.

I visited the island of Terschelling this summer. I saw the church where my great-grandparents must have worshiped. I saw dozens of Schaap graves in the cemetery by the church. I wandered on beaches where my ancestors must have walked. I felt the cold spray of the North Sea, just as they must have felt it. I saw farms they might have tilled, dunes they may have hiked.

I live in a whole different world than those Schaaps must have lived in. Back then, lots of islanders used to take horses down to the beach every day to look at what the sea rolled in. The North Sea is a horror to sailors. There were thousands of wrecks just off the banks of the island of Terschelling. Most every cemetery on the island has graves of seamen never identified, bodies that simply rolled up on the sand, dead at the murderous hands of the sea.

It's interesting to think about how those relatives I never met must have lived. It's interesting to stand in the church where they must have worshiped, to look at the pulpit they watched every week. But those people are gone. Nobody remembers them.

Nobody will remember us either after awhile. We all die. Maybe someday some guy will wander back to a little burg in the middle of the North American prairie and look strangely at a house where some long-forgotten great-grandparents once lived, at a basement where some ancestor used to write devotional books . . .

Today's passage is a look back at Moses' ancestors. At first glance, Moses' huge family tree seems kind of boring, doesn't it? It is, I guess, but to me it's very comforting to know that if everyone else forgets us once we're gone, God will not. If our tracks are wiped away as cleanly as the footprints I left this summer—like those of my ancestors'—on Terschelling's huge beach, at least I know that *God* will always know who I am and who my great-great grandparents are.

Imagine stumbling on a dead body while walking a beach and knowing there was no way of ever identifying it. But God knows. Somehow, God knows all of our names.

....

What a comfort it is to know that somehow you've got everything in hand, Lord. You know us by our names; you know our families; you know it all. You are our God, and we find comfort in knowing that you love us. Amen.

THE DUFFERS

....

Read Exodus 6:28-7:7

When they first approach Pharaoh, Moses and Aaron are well established in senior-citizen country—both of them over eighty. Isn't that something? You can't help wonder what a pair of old duffers are doing, throwing their weight around in Pharaoh's court when they ought to be out on the golf course.

You'd think the two of them would be relaxing in a condo on the Red Sea, a place with a sun porch, a billiard table in the social room, and a half-dozen shuffleboard courts. People work all their lives—they've got a right to soak up rays in those long, chaise lounges.

But apparently God didn't see it that way. In today's passage God says to Moses, "I have made you like God to Pharaoh."

What a statement! Can you imagine how many people would love to hear those words? But God doesn't choose just anyone—he chooses an eighty-year-old man and his eighty-three-year-old brother.

I think that if the Lord had told the twenty-year-old Moses that he'd make him like God, it might have been dangerous for everybody. When people are in their twenties, they sometimes tend to think of themselves as invincible. If you don't think so, watch a bunch of twenty-year-olds bloody each other at YMCA basketball. The twenty-year-old Moses would probably have lacked the wisdom and judgment to fill that role.

A forty-year-old Moses may have had difficulty with that role too. When people hit forty, they try like mad to prove they're not! If the Lord had told Moses he'd make him a God at forty, Moses would have tried too hard to fit the role and look the part. I can just imagine him getting his hair permed and wearing a braid of gold necklaces and a black, sleeveless T-shirt while he hammers a new Harley-Davidson through the gears. Besides, lest we forget, at forty Moses was a murderer.

Maybe the Lord chose to say what he did to Moses at eighty, because that was the best time to recharge Moses' batteries. Maybe at eighty, Moses needed all the encouragement he could get. Whatever the reason, here we've got two eighty-year-olds, a couple of old duffers in white shoes and flamingo shirts, standing in front of the most powerful of Egyptians, none other than Mr. P., telling him what he ought to do. It's incredible.

The Christian faith is strange that way, isn't it? The first of God's covenant people was Abram, a landless, second-class citizen considered pretty worthless by people in his society because he couldn't even drum up an heir.

But God chose lowly Abraham. And in Exodus, God chooses a couple of old gents to get his point across to Pharaoh. Odd, isn't it?

It's a pattern, I guess. Look at the carpenter's Son in the New Testament: all he's got is the shirt on his back; came into town on a mule, for pete's sake; and when he died, he didn't even have a spot in the local graveyard.

In the Christian faith, God gets the best roles. He's the hero. But the great miracle is, I think, that God uses each one of us, no matter how unlikely, to build the kingdom.

....

Make us instruments of your peace, Lord. It seems
sometimes as if we really aren't much of anything in
the world, but we know that you will equip members
of your family as you see fit. Help us
to do your will. Choose us to serve you.
In Jesus' name, Amen.

A SYMBOL, A TRICK, BREAKFAST, AND BLINDNESS

....

Read Exodus 7:8-13

Most literature teachers (like me) would say that finding symbols is a matter of learning to read between the lines. It's a skill, something you pick up in school. Pharaoh may well have had Egypt's best education, but in understanding symbols, I'd give him about a C-.

Try your skill on this little tale:

A dog with a bone in his mouth prances across a little bridge, stops in the middle, pokes his head over the edge, and sees his reflection in the pond beneath. What he sees is a dog with a bone. Angrily, he drops his bone and barks. Poor puppy loses it all.

Okay, now for our lesson in literature: The bone obviously symbolizes what we have, our possessions, our wealth. That sounds almost literary, doesn't it? Seemingly unconscious of his own wealth, the puppy greedily desires the riches of the enemy reflection, and, plop, all is lost.

Now, for the symbolism. The bone is a bone. But it's more. It's a symbol of what we own—and, oddly enough, what we sometimes don't treasure.

The staff-become-snake in today's reading is also a symbol. That is, it's a stick turned reptile (biblical scholars don't agree whether it's a snake or a kind of lizard), but it's more.

Moses, the leader of his people, holds the symbol of his leadership—the staff, the crook stick of a shepherd. But, when he throws it to the ground, it becomes a slithering, murderous, engorging reptile. All good literature students would certainly infer that the act symbolizes that Moses' own leadership ("I will make you like God," the Lord told him) will be as dangerous as a real live cobra to Mr. P.

Now remember, Pharaoh went to the Harvard of the Nile, so he knows about symbols. "You think I don't get the point?" he says. "Watch this." Then he conjures up his best magicians, who pull the same trick. How? Maybe they have some trained water moccasins who play dead. Maybe they're simply sorcerers who fool around with spirits.

Whatever their method, it works. And once his magicians' serpents are wiggling around on the palace floor, Pharaoh smirks. "Nice try, boys," he says to Moses and Aaron, "but you get the picture, don't you? You don't scare me."

I love what happens next. Ever see a picture of a boa constrictor swallowing a rat? They do it live. Perfectly disgusting, but then snakes don't make great house guests.

Moses' snake slowly breakfasts on Pharaoh's—slowly, of course, because you don't swallow anything whole without some concerted effort. The Bible doesn't say that Moses pointed at the demonstration and smiled. But I can't help but think that he did. After all, it must have taken the good guys' serpent some time to put away the Egyptian's best tricks.

Credit Pharaoh with some knowledge of literature maybe. But it seems to me that at this point he can't tell a symbol from a slap in the face. This time, he can't read between the lines.

When it comes to the big lesson, he misses the point completely. C-, at best, I figure, and maybe that's a gift.

....

Lord, thank you for another witness of your power and your strength. In story after story, we see your hand in the world of Moses. Help us to see it as clearly in our world. Amen.

LORD OF THE RING

....

Read Exodus 7:14-24

When we think about the fight the Lord wages through the plagues, it's probably more accurate to picture God as a skilled prize fighter than as a street brawler, swinging at random. Now I realize that neither of those images are going to please some people. It's popular to think of God as, say, Santa Claus, some sweet old man with a handful of bon-bons.

But the God of the Israelites is a God who gets angry when people don't pay attention. God offers the peace pipe to Pharaoh—time after time, in fact. But when Pharaoh sneers, Moses' God starts swinging. If you don't like the picture, maybe you'd better close the book.

Even though I'm a Protestant, and even though I think we ought to do a little better job of celebrating the Reformation in October, I wince at the job the Reformers did on some of northern Europe's great cathedrals. Because they thought that Roman Catholics actually worshiped the statues erected in some of their churches, Protestants stomped into those cathedrals and tore up or tore down whatever they considered ungodly, destroying in the process some of Europe's finest art. Their motives, of course, were fine. But throughout history a lot of ugliness has occurred for what appear to be good motives.

Still, as we think about the plagues, it might not be bad to think about the systematic way in which radical Protestants sought to destroy what they saw as the heresy of the Roman Catholic church of the time. One by one, they knocked out images, claiming they were false gods.

With the plagues, God Almighty does the same thing, only God does it in the right way and for the right motives. The Egyptians, remember, worshiped tons of different gods, most of them related to animals or nature. So God starts with the Nile.

The Nile River is to Egypt what corn is to Iowa—in fact, a whole lot more. Outside of the Nile river valley most of Egypt is a big sandbox. Each year, when it overflows, the Nile brings tons of rich soil to Egyptian land—"black land," Egyptians call it. In Moses' day, the Nile fed the people and made them rich. Is it any wonder that Egyptians, who worshiped natural phenomena, might make that river into a god?

But with the plagues, the God of Abraham and Jacob, of Moses and me, knocked down the Egyptian gods, one after the other, as if they were state fair Kewpie dolls. He started with the Nile, the most important physical feature of Egypt, and turned it rotten. Aaron stretched out his hand, and the water turned blood red. God made the Nile stink and turned its fish belly-up. A source of life became a source of death.

We'll see more of this as we go on into the other plagues, because the Lord has more in mind here than simply the people's release from slavery, as great as that might be. God is waging a full-fledged fight against an opponent who isn't as tough as he's cracked up to be.

Remember, this is the great I AM doing the swinging here, not some silly street thug. And God knows how to throw punches. God's the champion. "I AM the LORD," God keeps saying.

And God is not just shadowboxing. The gods that are getting beat up have a following the LORD wants, so the I AM is letting them have it, one at a time.

....

When we see your hand in our lives, the way you work, we wonder if it can be real. But we know you as God because you sent your Son for us; your Word became flesh in his life of love. Help us to pattern our lives after your pattern of love.
In his name, Amen.

STRONGLY FORBIDDEN TO LAUGH

....

Read Exodus 8:1-15

I have a little sign tacked to my wall, right here beside the desk where I'm typing. It's only three-by-five or so, printed on blue paper, sticky on the back. And it says in Dutch: *Streng verboden te lachen*, which means "strongly forbidden to laugh."

I'll probably never throw this fifty-year-old sign away. It's special to me because of its history. Hundreds of little slips of paper like this were printed by the Dutch underground during World War II. Most of them got used. A good friend of mine gave me this one, which didn't.

The Nazis really got into propaganda once they'd occupied a country. What they wanted more than anything was to convince the local people that they were all-right guys. So they'd put up posters asking people to join the cause—nice, big-shouldered posters with pictures of healthy men and women working hard for the Führer, Hitler.

Now the men and women from the underground, innocently strolling by these posters, would quickly lick these little signs (like the one pinned to my wall) and slap them up on the Nazi posters. Remember, what they say is "strongly forbidden to laugh." But that's not what they mean. They mean exactly the opposite. They're a joke really, a joke built on something called *irony*, which means "saying one thing but intending another." These little signs really beg folks to belly laugh, even though they tell them not to.

Nazis had a lot of trouble understanding that kind of joke because they were so driven by their desire to conquer the world and begin a master race. Because of their ambition, they lacked irony; in fact, they lacked a sense of humor. They could laugh at other people, but they couldn't laugh at themselves.

People who are driven often lack a sense of irony. Unfortunately, that includes a lot of Christians. Their eyes are so blinded by their sense of seeing God that they can't see themselves.

There's an old story about a boy who thought he had to become a preacher because one day out in the cornfield he saw clouds form a

"P.C." in the sky. He thought it meant "preach Christ." But the kid didn't have the brains of a box of rocks. His poor seminary teacher had to tell him that maybe "P.C." meant "pick corn." The boy was so filled with a vision, he couldn't see himself. He'd lost his ability to think clearly.

If any believer had a reason to be filled with a vision, it was Moses. How many people get bossed around by a burning bush, after all? But he never lost his sense of irony. "You don't like the frogs?" Moses says to Pharaoh. "Then you say 'when,' and God will call them off."

Moses puts Pharaoh, flooded with frogs, in the driver's seat—even though it's clear that Pharaoh, who thinks he's God, has zero power. "You say when," Moses says, "go ahead."

This could be Moses' flashiest move in this deadly poker game that he and Pharaoh are playing. "Tell you what," he says, "you just tell God when to call off these fat frogs."

I'll bet Moses could have laughed right then, right there in the palace, but I'm sure it would have been strongly forbidden.

But maybe we'll allow him a smirk. Just one.

....

Even at the moments when we think everything is going right and we don't even think of you, we know, Lord, that the world we live in—and everything we do—is in your control. What a glorious Savior we have! Amen.

MIRIAM'S STORY III

....

Read Exodus 8:12-15

I myself had to dig at the banks of the Nile, as if I were a child. Can you imagine that? I was nearly ninety years old, and I had to dig to get fresh water that wasn't red and thick like blood.

Then a week later it was frogs. When the Nile floods, you live with frogs. Their constant croaking drones into the night like some dream that won't slip back into silence. But what happened when Aaron lifted his rod that time was a hundred times worse. They were everywhere—in my bed and breadbox, in my closet, in my flour. They came up like a plague— horrible, fat, jumping things, with all their infernal noise. Stupid beasts, big bulging eyes, warty bodies, slimy, clumsy.

I was nearly ninety years old, and I had to kill them with my own hands. They sneaked into the house, seeped in like dust, and I swatted them with my broom. Fifty, at least, here in my home.

Moses sat calmly through all of this, as if he heard the sound of people criticizing, but not the words themselves. He knew something that we didn't. But he didn't smile.

Aaron *did* hear the words. Although Aaron was older than Moses, he was not as strong. When the anguish of our people rose to a point where Aaron began to question, he looked to Moses, who still sat, silent and knowing. But I could tell Aaron was nervous.

Do you understand how full of stench the air was during that time?

The river ran red and thick as mud. People stopped going there to gather water or to wash their clothes. The smell at the banks—it was overwhelming. In fact, it was almost more than a smell. It ate its way into your senses. It entered your nose, yes, but it also entered your eyes, turning them sore and red, and the thickness of the stench made you gag.

The frogs stank too—they almost drove some people crazy. Just when you thought that you'd gotten them all, that all of your frogs were gone, you'd find one fat one rotting beneath a table, behind a stool, in the corner of the room where you'd forgotten to look. And of course you wouldn't simply *find* it there; it wouldn't come as a surprise. You would be led by your nose—by this reeking, tainted foulness—and you would know that somewhere you had missed one. Look for it, eh! Find it fast or leave the house!

The streets were burning with stench. I saw people sweep frogs in piles from the alleyways. They lay in heaps, fly-besotted mounds. That was what we had lived with since my brother Moses had told Pharaoh that the Hebrews needed to go away to worship the Lord.

"Who needs this Lord?" my friend Elkinah said when my brothers were gone. "You ask them once, Miriam," Elkinah bellowed, "who of us wants to worship the god of dead frogs? Ask them that."

It did no good for me to say that Moses felt his strength came from the Lord, the God of Abraham and Isaac, the God of Joseph—not with a ton of rotting, stinking frogs in the street. So I sat in silence.

That afternoon my brothers returned and didn't speak—Aaron and Moses sat in my house and prayed, eyes downcast, as if whatever had happened had been an end to this burning bush in Midian. Moses himself closed the shutters over the windows, and the two of them, guests in my home, sat there as if waiting for a storm.

I didn't speak to either of them, not for hours.

Not until I saw the bugs—dozens of bugs, dozens and dozens.

Then I knew why, once again, they were both so quiet.

It was unbelievable, the whole situation. It's a story we must never forget.

....

It doesn't take plagues to make us forget to trust in your strength, Lord. It takes a whole lot less. Stay by our side, even when we forget that you're always there. In Jesus' name, Amen.

TONS OF BUGS

....

Read Exodus 8:16-19

Not even the sharpest biblical brain can say for sure what kind of bug Aaron brought out of the dust when he slapped it with his staff. Maybe lice, maybe mosquitoes, maybe gnats, maybe ticks.

Lice are tiny, but you can see them—if you're interested. They hang out in your hair and make their living by sucking blood. Kids often pick them up in school, even if they shampoo three times a day. If lice bite, they can cause infections; but for the most part, they're pretty harmless.

Mosquitoes are far *too* visible to most of us. In hot, humid weather they often breed rapidly and relentlessly. Sometimes mosquitoes carry malaria and encephalitis, which are no laughing matter. But mostly, mosquito bites are an itchy, ugly bother, not much more.

Gnats can be aggravating because they have a thing about ears. They're tiny flies, no bigger than eraser specks, and they've been known to bite—although almost anybody strong enough to breathe can fight off their worst attack. They're pesky and irritating, but they're usually about as dangerous as, say, bad breath.

Ticks are little round things that must be related to lice—at least in that they hitchhike and live on your blood. They're so small you have to look closely to find them, and the little buzzards have this awful habit of going for the darkest little corners of your body.

If I were Moses, and the Lord gave me options for bug warfare, I'd choose ticks. They're perfectly awful. They'll stick their heads into your skin and gorge themselves on your blood, sometimes growing to several times their natural size. Gross little vampires. When the skin around the bite gets hard, people get halos from these little horrors. Even worse, ticks carry Rocky Mountain spotted fever, and, as we all know today, Lyme's disease. Neither of those options are much to look forward to.

But the main reason I'd choose ticks if I were Moses is that you get ticks from good times. Lice you can pick up at school, mosquitoes bite anywhere, and gnats are in everybody's backyard. But, unless you live in the woods, you usually pick up ticks when you're doing something fun—like camping, or hiking, or picnicking.

Ticks are rotten spoilers. Get a cabin up north somewhere, do some fishing, a little water skiing, and some hiking. When you get home, you take a shower and tell yourself what a great time you had. That's when you find one of these little buggers looking for a spot to bed down.

They're dangerous, and they're party poopers. And that's why I like to think that they're the culprits who brought misery to the Egyptians.

What we know for sure is that the third plague's little buggers made the Egyptian magicians look like fools. For the first time, they couldn't duplicate what Aaron did with the staff. "Sorry, Mr. P.," they must have said.

Let's not forget what all these object lessons are about. God used the plagues to wake people up to the I AM, to make them aware that the LORD is God. Pharaoh didn't quite get the point yet, but the magicians, full of tick lumps, told him plainly, "We're sorry, boss, but this one belongs to some kind of god."

Of course, the whole story could have stopped right here. But Pharaoh was still just softening. It would take more than a tick to knock him down, a lot more. I just hope that he didn't get away clean on this one. I hope one of those little buggers started dining on some spot he couldn't see!

Lord, you own all of nature. You made it. Even ticks have their place in the world you've created. And you made us to rule your creation. Give us wisdom to know how to take care of your natural world, and give us awe to continue to love it because it reflects your presence. In Jesus' name, Amen.

WHEELING AND DEALING

····································

Read Exodus 8:20-31

Friday we painted the block walls off-white; Tuesday we bought a hunk of secondhand carpet and cut it to size. I ran a wire downstairs from the antenna and hooked up an old TV that suddenly flashed a pretty decent picture. The kids hauled down the VCR.

It was their idea, but I can't blame them. They wanted a room in the basement where they could bring their friends. The family room upstairs is too much in the middle of things, and besides, if their parents are around, their friends can actually *see* them.

What we still need is furniture. I gave them an old orange chair I had in my room here, one I picked up for a dollar at an auction. My daughter winced. Okay, so it's not a prize. But I told her it had a good foundation—solid oak. (I think that's like trying to tell her to go out with a kid who's really a nice boy!)

She's right, though, we need more furniture. We took our bikes to a furniture store in town, whose owner stores used furniture in a football field-sized warehouse—just in case some yahoos like us need an extra basement room.

We dug through the refuse and found a love seat with a red tag that said $75. My wife pulled up her nose—at both the price and the odor, I think. I tried to make a deal with the man in the furniture store, but he told us we'd have to barter with the *actual* owner. Apparently the furniture store doesn't own that love seat or any of the other treasures out there in Museum of Out-of-Date Furniture Design.

So I called the name on the tag, thinking they'd be happy to get rid of their old love seat for $25. My wife said to offer $40, just in case. So when a woman picked up phone, I offered $40.

"Oh, I paid *so much* for that," she said, "I just can't let it go for that little."

My heart was set on not a penny more. "Okay," I said, and hung up.

That was Saturday, last. I thought I'd try $50 Monday afternoon. I figured she'd be crazy not to sell. It wasn't worth $75!

What Pharaoh is doing with Moses in this passage is much like what I was doing by phone—bartering. And I think we're a lot alike—Pharaoh and me: at this point, we're both getting weak-kneed.

"If you need a vacation," Pharaoh says, slapping flies out of his face, "stay around home, all right? We can use the tourist dollars."

He's bartering, giving an inch maybe, but that's all.

I like Moses' tongue-in-cheek reply. "That's a generous gesture, Mr. P.," he says, "but if we'd stay around, you Egyptians wouldn't appreciate our enthusiasm." (He's right, of course. Jewish animal sacrifices would have made the Egyptian animal worshiper's blood boil.)

At least Pharaoh's made an offer. He's suffered through bloody rivers, carpets plush with frogs, and a Normandy-like invasion of ticks. Now he's got mega flies and no sticky paper. But at least he's finally negotiating.

Why is he so stubborn? Easy. Try to change the mind of a man who's been told since he was born that he was god. It's not easy for him to give in to a couple of old Hebrews packing a fancy shepherd's stick. It's tough backing off when you think you're god.

At least he's bartering now. But he's going to lose this one, just wait and see. You can't really bargain with the I AM.

Monday, my daughter still wanted the love seat. I figured I'd end up forking over the $75. But I sent her back to look at the color one more time to be sure.

She came back and said it was marked "sold."

Me and Pharaoh, huh?

....

We often find it difficult to give up things that are
important to us, Lord, even when we know that you
would rather that we do so. It's tough to give
ground, especially when our pride is at stake.
Forgive us, Lord, and help us give ourselves
to you. Amen.

WHY AND WOW

Read Exodus 9:1-7

The old Puritan Cotton Mather was a strange bird, but I sort of like the way he fooled around with science. In an essay written over four hundred years ago, he describes the scientific cause for lightning in some detail, and then cautions the reader that all this technical stuff shouldn't take away a bit from the fact that God still makes these heavenly booms.

> There is [God's] Voice most sensibly to be heard in the Thunder, Power belongeth unto God. There is nothing able to stand before those Lightnings, which are styled the Arrows of God. We see Castles fall, Metal melt, Bricks themselves vitrify; all flies, when hot Thunderbolts are scattered upon them.

What I like about this guy is that he describes what happens scientifically, but he doesn't lose his sense of awe. Even if he knows *why* something happens, he can still say "wow."

It doesn't always go that way. Let me give you an example. I have a confession. When I was a kid and heard these plague stories, I was sure that all of Egypt's water was turned to blood—really, B positive, A negative. The Bible said blood, and that's the way I pictured it.

But if you read that passage again, you'll find that clean water could be found simply by digging right along the bank. So was everything blood or not? Probably not.

The problem is, lots of the plagues can be understood if you know the habits of the Nile. For instance, when the river turned to "blood," it may have simply been turning red from Ethiopian clay. That happens—not every day, but it happens. Try to imagine that all of a sudden the Nile turned red and thick with clay, ketchup-like, flooded over, and left everybody in Egypt in shock. It could have happened.

Keep on going. Now just figure that maybe with that wild red flooding—something awful anyway—a hundred million frogs, like something out of Stephen King, came up out of the weeds and bounded into everybody's kitchens. That's not unlikely, is it? Weird things happen.

As long as we're this far, what about the bugs?

Sure?—why not. Water comes up high, frogs migrate, and flies and bugs breed by the dozens—swarms blacken the sky. Sure, makes sense.

Okay, smartie—what about this disease in the cattle?

No sweat—flies carry all kinds of germs. Today, any vet worth her keep would call it anthrax.

These things are all explainable, see? Maybe really strange things happened in Egypt, but nothing some sharp researcher couldn't explain.

But so what if all nine of God's opening shots can be explained by some scientist? So what? Moses still called them all, didn't he? Pharaoh must have gotten awfully sick of those two Hebrews raising that staff.

That's why I like old weird Cotton's way of looking at the facts. *So what* if all these miracles are possible to explain? *So what* if scientists can pin down every last plague to some rare natural phenomenon?

"So what?" I say.

"So what?" Cotton Mather would say. "Wow!"

....

Your creation is a wonder, Lord. What you've made,
we're still beginning to discover. How exactly you
made it, we may never know. But thank you
for giving power to us, your people.
In Jesus' name, Amen.

MIRIAM'S STORY IV

....
Read Exodus 9:8-12

Not all of that period before the deliverance was so horrible. We laughed sometimes too. My friend Elkinah laughed till her sides ached about the boils—big fat pimples on Pharaoh. How she laughed!

"You didn't laugh when you found frogs in your flour," I reminded her. "And when the Nile turned to blood, you wouldn't speak to me because of my brothers. When Pharaoh ordered the men to find their own straw, you never once showed your face in my kitchen."

Elkinah nodded in agreement, but kept laughing until the tears streamed down her face. "Oh, Miriam," she said, "are you so old you can't joke anymore? You saw them—some Egyptians can hardly move. Just awful is how they look—"

"Laughing at others' suffering—" I said, "—you think that's right?"

She sat beside me and tried not to laugh. Tried, but didn't succeed. Every time she'd calm herself, some crazy picture would pop into her mind. "Here, he has one," she said, pointing to her bottom, and she broke up again, all a bowl of wiggles, just like a child—a grown woman, barely able to sit up. "Imagine that, Miriam—Pharaoh, the great one, couldn't sit!" That's what she told me.

"Couldn't sit?" I said.

"On the throne!" she said, and she rolled her eyes, her face tight with laughing.

"Elkinah," I said, "for shame."

She burst into fierce laughing. "'More pillows!'" she screamed, as if there were a hundred eunuchs right there. "'More pillows, hurry!'" and she pointed again to you-know-where, this woman I call a friend.

I guess I knew why Elkinah could laugh now, even though she couldn't before. The Nile of blood was something we had never seen before, and the frogs were a bellowing nightmare—everywhere, you saw them. The gnats' infernal buzzing never stopped; it drove everyone crazy. But the Egyptians were the only ones whose cattle died and the only ones with boils. None of *us* were touched. I guess that's why Elkinah could laugh.

"What a blessing it is, Miriam, this Jewish blood," she said, wiping her eyes again. "What a blessing it is."

"What do you mean?" I said.

"No boils!" she said, and she pulled up her sleeve to show her spotless arm. "Not one, Miriam. Not one! No one in Goshen. Not one single boil. What wonderful blood!"

"Blood?" I said.

"Pure," she said, "not evil—like Egyptians' blood."

"No boils is a gift of the *Lord*," I told her. "This crazy idea about pure blood—where do you get such nonsense? God's favor we have, but no pure blood. What we have is a gift from God."

She looked at me strangely. "Maybe so," she said, wiping her face with the back of her hand, and then once again she started laughing. "But on his nose he has one, Miriam—did you hear? Big like the end of a finger. One on his bottom, one on his nose."

"This I don't believe," I said to her.

"Heeeeere," she wailed, and she pointed to the tip.

"On his nose too?" I said. "Surely not on his nose." I covered my mouth with my hanky to hide the grin growing there. I knew I shouldn't laugh, but I really couldn't hold it in anymore . . .

I had cried plenty during the past few weeks. Now I found I could laugh some too. It's all part of the story.

Lord, we thank you for the plagues—not for the suffering they brought to the Egyptians, but for the freedom they brought your people and the lessons of life they still bring to us today.
Amen.

THE SEVENTH PLAGUE

....

Read Exodus 9:13-33

Somewhere in the New Testament we read that the day of the Lord will come as a thief in the night. If that's true, we can assume quite safely that the Lord won't ride in a hailstorm chariot.

Out here where I live, where the prairie skies smile so wide you see almost forever, hailstorms, while not exactly proper gentlemen, at least announce their visits ahead of time, although not always courteously.

Imagine that it's summer, late in the afternoon. The western sky, a perfect shiny blue all day, begins to haze and darken, as if somewhere far away a sheet of dust hangs just beneath the sun.

An hour passes, the sun slips in silence beneath a ridge of darkness whose sharpened edges now appear like canyon walls. The wind slows, and a touchable thickness sits and waits in the air. In town, the streetlights come on, triggered by the darkness, and people stand in their backyards, looking west.

Lightning twists through blue-green clouds that swirl in sudden winds, often warm and wet. People watch for tails from those swirls, funnels that stretch to the ground and threaten to carry off corncribs, or worse, houses. Thunder shakes the windows. Cats hide under beds. Cattle swarm together.

Hail doesn't march in like a downpour. It sends spies: first, here and there, a clink, a crack—bouncing off the sidewalks. A hailstorm's firstfruits are often it's pride. Out here, they can be huge—baseball-sized; but when the storm really begins in earnest, when the hail falls thick as rain and beats the breath out of everything standing, it's not so large anymore.

It's not the baseballs that strip corn down to nothing but shards of wispy green. It's not golf balls that flatten soy beans. It's not the spies that ruin the wheat. It's the battalions of hail that follow that stomp everything. After a bad hailstorm, a white blanket lays over the ground like snow, long funnels stand like statues beneath the gutter spouts, leaves are left scattered over lawns.

So if Egypt is anything like Iowa, this world-class hailstorm Moses promised Pharaoh didn't come in like a thief in the night. It announced itself in a turbulent sky that, likely as not, Pharaoh and all his advisors must have watched brewing all day long. My favorite image of this seventh plague is Pharaoh standing outside, the way people do here in Iowa, just watching, in frightened powerlessness.

My goodness, by this time Pharaoh had to know that Moses was more than just lucky. He had to know that this kind of prophecy was something far beyond the ken of his best magicians. As he stood there on the palace veranda, he probably admitted to himself that what he was dealing with here was awesome supernatural power. He probably had hours to watch that monster grow as the bright afternoon shut down in darkness.

Maybe that's why he tells Moses now, for the first time, "I have sinned." Maybe that confession wasn't just another card played in this brutal game between Moses and Pharaoh. Maybe Pharaoh meant it.

But confessing error is not the same as confessing only one God. That's what the I AM wants: Pharaoh's own testimony. The God of creation wants belief from the god-king of Egypt.

God will get it. But it's going to cost Pharaoh so much more.

....

Sometimes we see you best in nature, Lord—on a
mountain's craggy sides, in the semi-darkness of an
ancient forest, beside a wide river. Thank you, Lord,
for appearing to us when you do. Help us to see you
in everything. Amen.

NOT SUCH A BAD GUY

....

Read Exodus 10:1-20

I was sitting in the mall a couple of nights ago, reading, waiting to meet my family. I was sitting there right by Orange Julius when these young guys walked by—three of them, sixteen, at most, all carrying Spencer's bags. I noticed them because they seemed to be in a hurry.

I glanced back at my book, but decided it was time to heed the call of nature. So I stuffed the book in my bag and hiked to the restrooms. Once inside, I saw these same three guys, bare-chested, changing into new T-shirts. All three had bought heavy-metal T-shirts—black, sleeveless, blazing with color—Guns 'N Roses or Motley Crüe or Skid Row or something. Really wild nightmare drawings.

They put the shirts on, stuffed the old ones in their sacks, then marched out into the mall. And you can bet they strutted their stuff. Once outside, they were big time. Macho.

Now I'm not stupid. I may be old, but I'm not stupid. I know what these guys want—image. They want to walk around as if they've got an attitude. They think the black, heavy-metal T-shirts paint the right picture—evil. The guys themselves are probably not evil—but they sure want to look that way.

Pharaoh probably wasn't as evil as he looks to you and me either. I know I've been saying some bad things about the guy, and he certainly wasn't anyone's favorite uncle. It's not too tough to imagine him strutting his stuff in a heavy-metal T-shirt. But he's not *only* evil. As a matter of fact, sadly enough, he's all too human. In some ways he's not much different from you or me.

Example. If you listened closely to today's passage, you might have heard him confess once more that he had sinned. Now how are we to take that? As just one big fat lie? *Sinned*? Pharaoh? The man must be speaking with a forked tongue.

I don't think so. When he says he's sorry, he means it. *When* he says it. Look what happens. Even his right-hand men beg him to give Moses what he wants. Living through bloody water, tons of frogs, flies, and ticks, a horrendous cattle disease, boils, killer hail, and now clouds of locusts must have been terrible. Destruction everywhere. Madness and mayhem. The locusts devour everything in sight.

"I have sinned," Pharaoh confesses. It's no lie. He's in the dumps—kind of like Marty . . .

Marty grabbed a whole roll of fishing line off the rack at Wal-Mart. When he stepped outside, a clerk nabbed him. He started to bawl. "I'm sorry, I'm sorry, I'm sorry," he said, tears bouncing off the sidewalk. Can't you see I'm sorry?"

The clerk seemed tired. "Pay up and you can go," he said.

Marty paid. Then he wiped his brow. "Shoot," he sighed. "I was almost cooked—almost." Then he shrugged his shoulders, laughed a little, and walked away. Free again. Wow—free again.

When we get caught red-handed, we're all sorry, aren't we? So was Pharaoh. He was terribly sorry when he saw locusts chew up what was left of fair Egypt. Sure he was sorry. Wouldn't you be?

But Marty walked off whistling, thinking he was lucky. And so does Pharaoh—once again.

He may be bad, but maybe he's not as evil as we'd like to think. He's not so much different from Marty—or us, for that matter. I can understand him. Can't you? Sure, he's sorry—for a while.

....

Dear Lord, sometimes confession is something we do to save our hides. Grant us forgiveness—and when our confessions are insincere, discipline our lives so that we look to you for grace.
In Jesus' name, Amen.

REVIEW DAY

....

Read Exodus 10:21-29

It's time for a review. But don't worry, there's no test tomorrow . . .

In the ninth plague darkness sweeps over the land, the last gasp before the monster that will end the negotiations between Moses and Pharaoh. As we take a closer look at this plague, we'll bump into some ideas and possibilities we've talked about before.

1. Bloody Water and Windy Darkness. Just like every other plague, this one—darkness so thick it can be felt—could have been predicted by a decent meteorologist and explained on the evening news. Some scholars feel that the same wind that loaded up the locusts and swept them away simply blew in sandstorms so thick you could feel the air. It happens. Sometimes for as long as fifty days the Egyptian skies fill with dust so heavy it blots out the power of the sun.

So, darkness-that-can-be-felt isn't a miracle? Wrong, it's a terrific miracle—not because it couldn't have happened otherwise but because God "managed" nature. Through Moses God outlined exactly what would happen to Pharaoh, then proceeded to walk him through the horrors.

Which brings this review to another old idea:

2. The Battle of the Gods. The bloody Nile was a bloody nose for one of the major gods in the Egyptians' religious museum. By taking on the Nile, God embarrassed the great river god, poked a finger in the Nile god's eye. That was number one.

Plague number nine takes on another major-league god—Amun-Ra, the sun god. This time, God puts shades on the whole country, hangs up a thick curtain in the sky. None other than Pharaoh himself was thought to be the incarnation of the Egyptian honcho god, Amun-Ra, so you can bet he really hated groping around in the darkness.

So what? The battle for the Israelites' freedom is really a battle between the many gods of Egypt and the I AM, Creator and Sustainer of the Universe. But then, it's not much of a battle—it's like the Yankees taking on your little sister's Pee-Wees.

All of which helps us to focus on another idea we've considered before:

3. The Art of the Bluff. Sometimes I've called what goes on between Moses and Pharaoh a poker game. If you don't like poker (there's lots of reasons not to), try chess. The point is, in this dialogue between the two of them, Pharaoh uses some tricky bluffs.

Already when he was flooded with frogs, he promised to let the Hebrews go. But once the croaking died, he changed his mind. When he was crawling with ticks, he told Moses the Hebrews could sacrifice to their God—as long as they stayed in Egypt. Moses didn't give in. When the hail beat the tar out of the crops, he actually told Moses that he'd sinned. But that wasn't enough. After the locusts, he told Moses the *men* could go. Moses politely declined. This time, in the darkness, Pharaoh tells Moses *everybody* can go—but he wants their animals. Who can blame him? After the cattle sickness, the market on beef likely shot out of this world.

But Moses isn't bargaining or making prudent financial moves, and he sure isn't bluffing. He's not interested in compromise. This isn't politics, this is war: the I AM versus Egypt's phony gods.

That's it for the review. Remember, there'll be no test tomorrow.

But, whether you knew it or not, there was one today—a big one, number nine. Guess what? The results are in: Pharaoh flunked royally.

....

Lord, help us to find ourselves in your Word. Help
us to know how to live, what to be, who to follow.
Thank you for the stories of your people.
Thank you for the witness they give.
In Jesus' name, Amen.

BULLYING DEATH

....

Read Exodus 11:1-10

You can't blame the Egyptians for holding a grudge against death, because you don't have to be heathen to dislike dying. But the Egyptians hated death with a passion. That's why they knocked themselves out building the pyramids.

Egypt's *Great Pyramid*, located at Giza, near Cairo, stands four hundred fifty feet (130 meters) high. That's as tall as a forty-five-story building. The pyramid's base covers thirteen acres, roughly ten football fields.

Now if you figure that this mighty pyramid was built more than four thousand years ago, you'll understand that this huge thing couldn't have been constructed with sky-high cranes and hydraulic elevators. No way. Sweat—and blood, too, I'm sure—built the pyramids.

How much? That's anyone's guess, I suppose. Some people claim years and years of work with a gang of one hundred thousand, but who knows? We do know this: The Great Pyramid has 2,500,000 stones, all of them hand-carved, of course, by copper chisels and saws (there were no power drills back then), all of those boulders hoisted up to those unbelievable heights by an elaborate system of paths.

Here's the kicker. Each one of those two and a half million stones weigh better than two tons (that's 4000 pounds!). Do you know how many Arnold Schwarzeneggers it would take to manhandle two tons of limestone? My guess is at least a couple dozen, but that's only a guess.

Some of those boulders came from quarries nearby, but others were transported long distances. Once the stones were at the pyramid site, the slaves would drag them up long ramps to the layers they were working on that year. When they'd finish a layer, they'd rebuild the ramp to swoop higher.

More than two tons! I bet our *garage* doesn't weigh that much. Shoot!—a brand-new Probe GT turbo weighs in just a few ounces over 3000 pounds. You have to think in terms of a four-wheeler, say an SLT Lariat Workhorse, to get close to imagining the weight of one pyramid block. And, remember, the Great Pyramid contains *two and a half million* of those back-breakers.

Why? Simple—Death. The Egyptians hated death worse than a dry Nile bed. The pyramids are, after all, nothing more than the biggest burial vaults in the world. They exist yet today, almost five thousand years later, as memorials to people whose names have long ago been erased by time itself.

Funeral ceremonies were held inside these huge tombs, and sometimes a smaller pyramid for the queen stood right beside the head honcho's. And, of course, inside there was plenty of room for all the loot. Anthropologists have found whole rooms full of ancient Egyptian treasures that the Pharaohs stuck away for post-mortem partying.

The pyramids were built because the Egyptians felt that a person's body had to be preserved and protected in order for the soul to live. They were built, in other words, to avoid death— to preserve life.

The big plague, number ten, hit the Egyptians right where it hurt. It brought death to their doorstep, made dying as common as slave labor. It simply rubbed out another staple of Egyptian faith and life.

Death comes, period. No one tried harder to keep it away than the ancient Egyptians did. That may be at least part of the reason why the I AM chose the death of the Egyptians as the deliverance for the Israelites.

But what a terrible, terrible night!

....

Sometimes when we fear dying, Lord, we forget that
there is no death with you as our Savior. Your blood
on the cross frees us from our slavery.
Thank you for deliverance. Amen.

QUIRKY CULTURES

....

Read Exodus 11:4-6

I'd like someone to explain to me why the television show *Dallas* was such a huge success in West Germany, but failed in Japan.

I'd also like to know why the ordinary Alaskan buys more flowers in a year than an ordinary citizen of any other state. Is that because not as many flowers grow up north—or are Alaskans just a little more romantic than the rest of us?

And what about the Peul women of Mali? Why do they tote their valuables in earrings the size of handbags instead of using purses like other women do? Don't those earrings hurt?

If you dig around a little, all kinds of surprising "people facts" start jumping out at you. Take a look at these:

- A typical Argentinean eats twice as much meat, per year, as a typical North American. (Good night, that's a lot of burgers!)
- One hundred years ago, English aristocrats served only two foods on a napkin: ice cream, and—get this—asparagus.
- In Southeast Asia people often stored their pearls in pairs, thinking—well, hoping, I suppose—that those pearls would wait for the right moment and mate.

Weird words can be fun to think about too. For example, If you order "broccoli" in England, you get "cauliflower," and what we call "Danish" is "Vienna Toast" in Denmark. I was born in a state where most people call water fountains "bubblers," and where at picnics kids drink "soda water," not pop or soda.

Why? Who knows?

In Egypt at Moses' time, people thought the firstborn son was more important than the other kids. Again, I'm not sure why (just as I'm not sure why the Thong people of Vietnam loved to eat poultry—with the feathers on). For some reason, the firstborn was just considered most blessed.

(I might just assert here that *I* think it's not a bad idea—after all, I'm the firstborn son myself. But my two older sisters would probably consider such an idea just as wacky as the fact that some African bushmen don't talk once the sun goes down!)

It's the business of anthropologists to figure out why such quirky ideas manifest themselves in every culture of the world. For some reason, the ancient Egyptians—and the Hebrews—believed a father's dreams were made flesh in his firstborn son, so that if I were Egyptian, I'd receive a double share of inheritance—just because I was the firstborn boy. If the firstborn son were to die before his parents—say in some freaky accident or by some sudden sickness—the pain, strangely enough, was also twice as great for parents. It's odd, unexplainable, but true.

What I think is most interesting here, however, is that God knew all of this. When God chose to free the Israelite people and manifest the name of the I AM as the God of gods, he knew how to make the point stick with the Egyptians. God could speak their language.

See, the I AM is not the I WAS. The I AM is eternally "with it." Today God knows about Air Jordans, TV sitcoms, and fluorescent windshield wipers. God knows our culture—and every other culture in the world.

The I AM knows ancient Egyptians and Medieval Europeans and twentieth-century Canadians. Hey, trust me, God knows. And the miracle is, God loves all of us.

....

Sometimes we think of you as our personal Savior—and you are, Lord. But you're also in all places at all times. You're the personal Savior of millions of people of all colors. Only you are God, and we thank you forever because you love us.
In Christ's name, Amen.

MIRIAM'S STORY V

....

Read Exodus 12:1-12

I will try to explain exactly what it was I felt on that night so long ago. It was as if I were on a path—on a path in the desert that leads to a cliff; and when I tried to see what lay ahead, I discovered I had been blinded. There was nothing there. A haze lay over that steep cliff, and I feared that I would fall. *Everyone* was scared, but that is what I felt.

And yet even in that frightening vision there was hope. Somehow I knew that even if I fell, I would feel the Lord's right arm beneath me like the wings of an eagle. The Lord our God would keep me from death—I knew that. But I was afraid.

I stood at my doorpost making the sign of the blood of the lamb on my house. Blood is not the juice of berries. Blood is not a dye. Blood is blood, and I smelled it there, in the jug. I can still feel its peculiar touch on my fingers. Blood carries life. I splashed blood on the doorpost, and it ran like water down the side of the house—ran in long red lines to the earth. The blood of the lamb.

We ate the lamb, too, as Moses commanded. We had chosen the animal carefully so he would be without blemish. We had pampered him, as we were told. He lived with us, in the house. And that night, we killed him. Moses said the Lord told him that it must be done—just this way.

There were no unbelievers that night. What Moses had done with his raised arm, what my brothers had done to the Egyptians, had silenced all of us. We waited. My brother Moses told us what this God of the burning bush wanted with us, this God who claims us, even today, as chosen people.

Up and down the street the houses were spotted and swathed with blood on the mantels. I saw my neighbor Elkinah outside, her straw broom in hand. She held the blood up high and reached in the jug with the broom. She didn't wait for the blood to drip from the straw—she splashed it on the doorpost, threw it over the house. God would not miss her mark.

The blood was a badge, a sign of life. The blood said that God would deliver us. Moses had said that this was the day the Lord had made for us, that everything was new. He reminded us that we were God's people—those of us who had this lamb's blood on the doorpost. We were the people who bore God's name.

But I was afraid anyway. Death came into that night like something not seen, only felt—it came like a thief, in silence. But when the angel passed through our streets and saw the sign on our doorposts, he knew that we were God's people. So he moved on in silence, the way he had come.

I was afraid, but I had hope. As I ate the lamb and dressed to leave, I knew I AM would be with me. I would be safe in God's arms—even if I walked over the cliff . . .

That's what it was like that night.

When trouble surrounds us, when it seems there's no one who cares, no one to take our part, you will be there, Lord, because you always have been there for those you love. Thank you for our deliverance through your Son. Amen.

SIN'S GERMS

....

Read Exodus 12:12-20

Tabitha has just finished dance-line practice. She and the other members of her dance team are getting ready for their number at the big home game on Friday night. They're doing a new routine from the Beach Boys, all dolled up in sunglasses and tank tops like real California girls. It's sure to be their best routine ever!

So as Tabitha and the other dancers walk down the hallway from the gym to pick up their books, they're laughing and talking together loudly. Up ahead they see Nancy and pause to give each other a few meaningful glances. As usual, Nancy's hair is a disaster. She wears thick glasses like you wouldn't believe and is crouched down on all fours—rump up like a hump—in front of her locker.

When they walk by her, no one from the dance line even says boo. I mean, Nancy is like from another world or something—you know? To the dance team, Nancy is almost dirt.

The thing is, Tabitha used to be Nancy's friend, her only friend. They grew up together. But today Tabitha dances on the team; Nancy just works on computers—she types up copy other people write for the school paper.

Sherry Witt's another story. Everybody loves her. And when Tabitha walks back from her locker, she's with Sherry—and Nancy Nerd is still down on all fours, trying to find her calculator or something weird like that. Long ago already Tabitha figured if she was going to get anywhere in school she would have to swear off knowing Nancy. She had to act as if Nancy Nerd had bubonic plague.

So she does. She pretends it's just the two of them, glorious Sherry and Tabitha. And although she knows Nancy is smiling, looking up at her longingly, Tabitha ignores her. I mean, she's got her reputation to look after, you know? What's left if you lose your reputation?

Leaven. God gives sharp commands concerning leaven in the passage you read today. Leaven is like yeast, a kind of germ. God says it's not to be used in the bread the Hebrews eat when they celebrate this incredible death-defying event that is about to occur.

Leaven works in bread the way sin can work in us. Once it burrows into the way we conduct our lives, it builds a nest, makes itself comfortable, grows like a tapeworm, and then refuses to leave.

Tabitha started shunning her childhood buddy when she realized that Nancy didn't fit in. After a while, it got easy. She could walk by, nose high, and not even feel guilty. Sin got comfortable.

When the Hebrews made bread in a kneading trough, they often left little chunks of the dough behind, chunks that contained leaven. They'd use these little bits of dough for the new bread, and that leaven would get in and work its power. Old leaven got into the new bread.

"Start over," God told the Hebrews. "Use some kind of Brillo on those kneading troughs, because I don't want any of yesterday's comfortable sin rising up out of the bread of your new lives. Everything's new. You've got a brand-new life as of this night. Set your watch!"

....

Our stubbornest sins, Lord, are the ones we don't see because sometimes we don't want to. We want other things more—popularity, money, a good front. Help us to love, not to hate. Break down the walls we put up. Keep our lives from being leavened with the old sins. In Jesus' name, Amen.

LOOKING AHEAD

....

Read Exodus 12:21-23

I guarantee that the story I am about to tell you will be the worst story ever written.

When they were seven, Nancy and Tabitha had a Kool-Aid stand out at the side of the street all summer long. At ten, they took the city bus to the pool every summer day for swimming lessons. But when they got into high school, everything changed. Tabitha got on the pom line, and Nancy's interests started and ended with a switch on a computer.

For most of her high school years, Nancy watched as Tabitha, her old friend, walked by her as if she were dead. She wasn't, of course, but their friendship was.

A year after graduation, Nancy was coming home from the University when she saw Tabitha slumped over behind the wheel of her car. She didn't know what was wrong, so she went over to the car and knocked on the window. When Tabitha looked up, her eyes were full of tears.

Nancy signalled with her hands to get Tabitha to open the window, but Tabitha seemed unable to move. So Nancy yelled, "Can I help you?"

Tabitha looked up at her old friend, the person she had ignored for the past five years, and she shook her head feebly, yes.

Nancy stepped back quickly, delighted to be able to help her old childhood chum. Unfortunately, stepping back from the car placed her right in the path of a kid humming along on his ten-speed. He smacked into her so hard that she broke a leg, sprained an ankle, and put a scar the size of a garter snake down her left arm.

I told you you'd hate that story, and I can even tell you why. It's because you're simply not prepared for the stupid ending. The guy comes along on a bike, and wham! Where'd the silly bike come from anyway? It's not hinted at anywhere in the story. Now if I'd have told you that Nancy dodged three cars and a motorcycle in order to get to

Tabitha's car, at least I'd have prepared you for that dumb ending. But I didn't. So you're right: the kid on the bike comes in out of nowhere.

If one of my students would write a story that bad, I'd tell her that if she wants to end it in such an awful way, she has to foreshadow the ending—that is, she has to hint at it somehow, give us some clues. That way, we might not like the story, but at least we could say it makes sense—sort of. We could say we were prepared for the ending. It may have been dumb, but at least it was foreshadowed.

Today's passage helps prepare us for something to come. The great Jewish ritual of the Passover foreshadows none other than Jesus Christ our Savior and his deliverance of us, his people. Christ is, after all, often referred to as a lamb in the Bible, and, just like the lamb of the Passover meal, Christ didn't have a spot on him. The blood on the doorpost, like Christ's blood on us, keeps his children from eternal death. And, like the ancient Hebrews, we have to believe that Christ's blood on our doorposts will mean what he says it will mean.

Because of what they foreshadow, these three verses are at the very heart of one of the most significant passages of the entire Bible. This blessed meal of the Hebrews prepares us, God's people, for Jesus Christ's death and resurrection. It's all part of the same story—the good news of the gospel.

Sometimes the Bible seems like a miracle itself. When we see how this story relates to the story of Jesus, it seems so much more wonderful. Thank you for your Word, your story. Amen.

RED AND YELLOW,
BLACK AND WHITE

....

Read Exodus 12:24-29

Something really great happened last night. At least I think it's great
because I love baseball. If you don't, I guess you might disagree.

Wilson Alvarez got called up to the big leagues just a day before his
first start with the Chicago White Sox. The Sox were in Baltimore for a
game with the Orioles, and Alvarez, who'd had ten wins and six losses
with a minor-league club in Birmingham, got the call.

He walked five hitters, so the game wasn't exactly a masterpiece,
but it was closer to perfection than most big-time chuckers ever get.
You know why? Because Wilson Alvarez, a Venezuelan native, in his
first major-league start this year, threw a no-hitter. A rookie with a no-
hitter!

I don't care—*I* call that a great story.

Alvarez, who's only 21 years old, is obviously a kid with talent. He
may never again fire a perfect game, but his potential has already
been proven. He's gifted, undoubtedly. He's been blessed with talents
that not everybody gets blessed with, even though thousands wish
they were. Alvarez, the kid, will get in the record book.

Wouldn't it be great to have that kind of ability, to be blessed with
that kind of talent? Of course, I admire anybody who can do things I
can't. I think of car mechanics as sheer geniuses, finish carpenters as
real artists.

We all have different talents, I guess. Some people say they'd
rather go to the dentist than write devotionals. I know people who'd
rather die than stand up in front of a crowd.

But what's great about God's love is that you don't have to throw
no-hitters to earn a star. You don't have to carve statues or practice
brain surgery. You don't have to raise the perfect family, write grand
opera, look like Madonna, sing like Paula Abdul, or chuck strikes like
Wilson Alvarez or Nolan Ryan. God loves all of us—and doesn't give
two hoots about how smart we are, how special we look, or how silly
we act. Besides, God's the only one I know who's really color-blind.

The blood on the doorpost is all the angels of God had to see, and they hurdled the place, passed right on by. They didn't look inside, didn't check for beautiful eyes or a sparkling personality. They didn't care—carpenters or catatonics; butchers, bakers, or candlestick makers.

All they needed to see was the blood on the door, and they moved on.

Here's what's special about God's love—both to the Hebrews in Egypt and to God's people today: It doesn't have diddly to do with us. We don't earn it by our looks or by our leaping. Salvation is free, scot free. All we have to do is believe that Christ's blood will save us.

That's it. Incredible.

....

Lord, everybody in our world cares about looks or
personality or athletic ability. It's so great to know
that none of that means anything to you.
All you want is our praise, our thanks.
Thank you, Lord. Amen.

THAT BAD OLD MAN

....

Read Exodus 12:24-28

My grandfather and I learned a little different Heidelberg Catechism than my kids learn. Here's what an old *Psalter Hymnal* says for question and answer 89:

Q. What is the mortification of the old man?
A. It is heartfelt sorrow that we have provoked God by our sins, and more and more to hate them and flee from them.

Okay, so maybe that sounds a little archaic. Maybe kids today don't understand *mortification, provoked,* or even *flee.* Whatever the reasons, we've changed the words a little in the hymnal my kids read:

Q. What is the dying-away of the old self?
A. It is to be genuinely sorry for sin, to hate it more and more, and to run away from it.

There's more than one difference here, of course, but noticeably absent, I think, is "the old man." What was "the old man" to my grandpa and me is now "the old self" to my kids.

I understand the reason for the change. Gone is gender. What's evil in us is no longer male. Instead, we just say "the old self." That's nice—but I still prefer the old wording.

Now I don't want to be crotchety, and the last thing I want to do is offend the boys down on the shuffleboard courts in south Florida, because the truth is, old women can be as sinful as old men, or—for that matter, young women or young men. Maybe old men *have* been getting the bad rap here. But I still like those words "old man of sin." While it's hard for me to imagine what an "old self" looks like, long ago already I had a cartoon picture (a vile one) in my mind of what the "old man" looks like:

He's warty, bent over in the shape of hedgehog, and he hangs out around porno shops. He's got a brand-new Sony camcorder in his car, just waiting to use on little kids he picks up when he promises them a Milky Way. His best laugh sounds ratchety and feels like a bad itch.

He's got spit in the corners of his lips, and when he talks his tongue lolls. He's not just an old man—he's a dirty old man.

What's worse, he's in all of us. If you don't think you've got him in you somewhere, you're lying to yourself. Not all of us are porn freaks, of course; that's not the point. The point is that all of us have a slobbering sinner in us, just as ugly as that greaseball on the sidewalk.

And the catechism says this guy's got to die. That's right. He's got to go, period. Repentance or conversion means he gets rubbed out.

The deliverance of Israel, that which we've been reading about now for so long, is no Disneyland dream. It's a glorious liberation for the Egyptian slaves, true, but it's got its downside. People—lots of them—suffer and die. Blood is shed. In the process of deliverance, the perfect lamb is slain so his blood can be splashed on the doorpost. Egyptians die by the hundreds to make the I AM's final, bloody argument stick forever.

And in the process of our salvation, this warty old man of sin that's in every last one of us—old guys and young gals—has to die. That's painful, but it's got to happen—and only Christ can pull it off.

The next question is, "What is the coming-to-life of the new self?" Answer: "It is wholehearted joy in God through Christ, a delight to do every kind of good."

Deliverance costs, but, my word, it pays!

....

Lord Jesus, the toughest thing for us to do is deal with our own sin, to look at ourselves closely, and to try to change. Something in us has to die before we can become pure. Wash us, Lord. Make us whiter than snow. Amen.

AN UNNATURAL NIGHT

....

Read Exodus 12:29-30

For all kinds of reasons, Macbeth shouldn't have shoved the dagger to Duncan. After all, Duncan was his king. Furthermore, on the night of the murder, Duncan was Macbeth's guest. In Shakespeare's world, and the world of Macbeth, both of these facts created sacred obligations.

But Macbeth, prompted by his own envy as well as his wife's, slipped out in the middle of a grisly night and killed his sleeping king. According to Shakespeare, who of course wrote the play, it was a most unnatural act.

In Act II, scene IV, an old man explains just how unnatural it was:
> *Threescore and ten I can remember well*
> *Within the volume of which time I have seen*
> *Hours dreadful and things strange, but this sore night*
> *Hath trifled former knowings.*

If you like poetry at all, you can't help but love the word *trifle* here. All the horror this old man has seen in his life, he says, was made silly by what he saw that night—and he never even witnessed the murder.

Another character in the play, young Ross, then tells the old man that whatever's been done isn't over. Even as they speak, the sun seems draped by some horrendous cloud, bringing darkness where there should be dawn.

"Tis *unnatural*," the old man says, "even like the deed that's done."

We are at the point in the story of the exodus which is most foul and most unnatural. And I think it is wrong to simply fly over it, as if the bad guys merely got what was coming to them.

I know that these words are being read in families where children have died, whether by disease or accident. I remember being told years ago that the greatest horror someone can suffer in life is the death of a child. I haven't experienced that horror myself, but I've heard it explained that way.

It is natural to bury your parents. Parents are older than children. Someday I fully expect to have to bury mine, as they did theirs before me. That expectation will make the task easier to do—even though, God knows, I don't look forward to it. The fact is, most of us will have to suffer the deaths of our parents.

But burying a child is most unnatural. No one is prepared by the natural process of aging to bury a child he or she has brought to life. We have no way of foreseeing such a death—no clear expectations. Therefore, no pain reaches as deeply as seeing children die. Even as I sit here in my basement, I know these words will be read by some moms and dads who have suffered this horror. Some right now are likely close to tears—just reading this. That's how real this horror is.

The tenth plague that beset the Egyptians leads Pharaoh finally to do what he should have done weeks ago: he tells the Hebrews to leave. What God has done is an extremely painful thing; he's taken a child out of every home in Egypt. Can you imagine the wailing in that world that night?

Now don't ever forget this. God knows that horror. God Almighty who brought this horror of horrors on the Egyptians understands perfectly.

You know why? Of course you do. Because God is a Father. And his Son, Jesus Christ, died unnaturally. God buried his Son for us. He knows.

....

It's really hard for us to understand the love of One who would allow his own child to die so that his creation might live. That's how great your love is, Lord, and that's why we thank you every day. Amen.

A TECHNICAL CLIMAX

....

Read Exodus 12:31-32

Here's the skeleton of the kind of story people love to watch:

Alex is a rich old coot, who has scads of cash he never spends. He never married, so he has no children to inherit all the dough. What he's got, however, are three nephews—Huey, Duey, and Luey—and they're all hungry. One night Alex is found dead, a napkin jammed in his mouth. The detective, a woman named Moose, thinks she smells some kind of foul play.

Huey bawls his head off when he hears poor unc is dead and gone, and he claims he was watching a movie when the murder happened—good show, he says. Duey says he was at the mall picking out a suit. Luey was off at the horse races, he says. All three of them shed crocodile tears.

Now Moose may be no looker, but she's right there with Columbo when it comes to deduction. When she scours the apartment once more for some kind of clue, she finds a ticket stub from the theater complex. It's in the vestibule, as if it fell from a coat pocket. The date stamped on the ticket puts poor Huey at unc's place—after the movie.

She's got him there at the scene of the crime, and she's got motive. But when she goes to pick up Huey, he takes off. What follows is a humongous car chase that ends with Huey's MG rocketing into a fourth-story window of the Empire State Building, turning New York into a sea of flame. Moose shakes her head as she gets out of her patrol car.

The credits roll.

There's a point to all this madness, and it has to do with the way stories—all stories—are built. Most of you know what a story's climax is: it's normally thought of as that moment, at the end, when things get really wild—cars crash, outlaws die.

What you might not know is that most stories actually have two climaxes—one, the *dramatic climax*, is the one everybody thinks about; the second, the *technical climax*, is a little more subtle.

In *Moose's Great Adventure,* as I related it above, the *technical climax* occurs at the moment Moose finds the theater ticket. It's at that point that Moose knows—and we know, if we're sharp—exactly how the story will end. Huey's goose is cooked once Moose scoops that ticket stub off the floor. The *dramatic climax* occurs when the MG piles into the Empire State Building and Manhattan goes up in smoke. The dramatic climax is the wildest point of most "drama," of course—the big boom that the audience remembers.

I say all of this because we've now come to the technical climax of the exodus story. It occurs in one line you've read for today: Pharaoh says, "Take your flocks and herds, as you have said, and go." Then he adds the request that stands as the "technical climax" of the story: "and bless me."

Really, the story is over. Way back when we talked about the real drama here being between the gods of the Egyptians—hundreds of them—and the one God of heaven and earth—the I AM. While Pharaoh has confessed his sin before, he's never acknowledged exactly what the Lord wanted him to—that the Lord God who Moses served is really the God of the universe.

Here, at the moment of death in his family and every household of Egypt, Pharaoh finally confesses that he needs the blessing of this God—not just any god, but *this* God. For the first time, Pharaoh's on his knees.

Does it make him a great believer? Nope. After all, he turns right around and orders his legions after the long columns of Hebrews moving out into the desert.

But when he asks Moses to bless him, the story is over. The battle we've watched for so long is now history. The I AM is the uncontested champion.

So technically, we might say, the story is over.

But, hang onto your hats, folks, because we've still got the chariot chase!

....

We know that people have worshiped different gods
for centuries, Lord, but we also know that you are
the only true God, the God who given us his Word.
Thank you for such a great gift. Amen.

MIRIAM'S STORY VI

....

Read Exodus 12:33-42

I was old enough, of course, to know that my little brother might be killed for nothing more or less than crying. In those weeks that I sat with him at night, I understood my parents' fear.

But I wondered how my mother could put such faith in a tar-box basket, how she could be so sure that Pharaoh's daughter would take my brother from the water and send me home again with him. I didn't know how my mother could be so sure things would turn out right.

I must tell you, in life many things happen that we don't understand. And sometimes they happen so far from our control that you can't help but know that God acts for us—not just in some things, but in everything. Why this God loves me, I don't know. All I know is that once God gave me my brother's life and now this same God gave all my people life. We were free! We were marching out of Egypt into freedom.

Someone holds our lives in loving hands, my friends. That someone is the Lord of the burning bush, the one Moses called "I AM." God's hands hold our lives. This story proves it too.

We knew all of that, and that was why we were walking in silence. The people whispered in huddled groups as we moved over the desert's carpet—so many hundreds and thousands of us.

No one spoke because although we had our freedom, and although we were leaving the land of our captivity, our oppressors behind us, we had done nothing ourselves. If all the Hebrews had stood in rebellion, had stormed Pharaoh's gates and killed his legions, we would have been triumphant as we walked. Our voices would have been raised in song.

But *we* had done nothing. The bloody battle had been fought in Egyptian homes, and everywhere the firstborn lay dead. Tonight, every Egyptian family wept for sudden, unexplained loss.

And in that war, not one of the Hebrews—not one of my people—raised so much as a hand. No one wielded a sword. Our arms were heavy with Egyptian bracelets. We moved into the desert with more money than any of us had ever seen, just as Moses had said. We were not the vanquished. We were not destroyed. We were the victors—but the victory belonged to our God.

That is why we walked in a kind of silence, in a reverence, in awe that confessed that what had happened to us was not done with our hands but with the Lord's. We were powerless. We were powerful in might and wealth, but our strength lay only in the Lord. This is the lesson of the exodus—and this must be our song forever and ever.

Praise be to God's name, for the I AM has won the victory!

....

O God, our help in ages past, our hope for years to come, be thou our guide while troubles last, and our eternal home. Amen.

TALK IS CHEAP

Read Exodus 12:43-51

Bryan joined the Flaggs, a street gang tighter than a fist. He got in because he was a mountain, big as a linebacker, arms like thick ropes. The Flaggs had this creed—they all stuck together, see? If some other gang came along and messed around on their turf, they dropped everything and went after them.

Bryan really got heated about the other gangs in the area. Sometimes he'd scream about going over across Wentworth and busting heads. Once he claimed somebody from the Dales, another gang, beat up on his girl just because they knew she was his girl. He was always spitting about fighting.

But when it came down to the nitty gritty, Bryan was always out to lunch somewhere. He could talk a mean fight, but if somebody needed help, Bryan was never around.

Soon enough the other Flaggs started talking about Bryan behind his back. They said they wanted to dump him because even though he was a great talker, talk is cheap.

It is, isn't it?

When I was sixteen, a buddy of mine worked on a construction gang with an elder from our church. My friend was shocked to hear the elder cuss just like the rest of the guys. It's not that my buddy couldn't let out some steamy words himself; it's just that at sixteen, neither he nor I expected it from someone we thought everybody considered saintly. To me, that elder's talk was cheap.

There's another side to the story, too, of course—after all, people say "the pen is mightier than the sword." But for right now, I want you to think about the fact that, often as not, talk is cheap.

How about this? I have to speak in Toronto next year—I have to talk about writing these kinds of meditations. So imagine that I fly into Toronto, and because I'm a U.S. citizen, my bags are searched. Some shaggy dog smells dope, because I've got enough cocaine in my clean socks to make me a hundred thousand dollars. And I've also got a Canadian customs guy standing over me with handcuffs.

Let's say it happens. What on earth are you going to do with this very book? My guess is, you'll trash it quick—this one and just about any other by James C. Schaap. Why? Because my words wouldn't be worth a whole lot anymore: "Christian writer smuggles cocaine."

What I like about today's passage, this discussion of dealing with outsiders, is that nobody says much. No angel steps into a front room and asks people to talk about doctrine. The blood is the whole story.

Now, those characters the Bible describes as "many other people"—which is to say, people who aren't Hebrews—simply have to be dealt with. What's going to happen to them? They're outsiders.

The answer is simple—just like the blood on the doorpost. If you want to be "insiders," talk is cheap. You've got to be circumcised, the Bible says. You've got to act. You don't have to say a word—you've just got to do.

In my church family today, there's endless talk about whether women should be preachers and about how God created the world. Lots of talk. Reams of paper.

If you wanted to be a part of the family of God traveling through the desert behind the pillar of smoke, you had to act. Talk is cheap.

....

Dear Lord, help us to act—not to play a part, but to be your people in everything we do, every day of our lives. And forgive us when we fail. In Jesus' name, Amen.

FIRSTFRUITS

....

Read Exodus 13:1-16

Here's the sad truth.

I asked my daughter to look through all our slides for old pictures. My parents were having their fiftieth anniversary, and I thought a cartoon slide show would be a scream.

So she did. She found shots at the zoo, at the beach, in the bathtub, at the park—tons of old pictures. Years ago I bought a really expensive camera and snapped away as if the world were running out of film.

Today, that camera sits in the closet. I used it this summer when we went to Europe—but otherwise that camera barely gets off the shelf. Once the newness wore off, I stopped snapping pictures of my nephews and nieces. So we've got dozens of pictures of the oldest kids, but barely a shot of the youngest.

Andrea picked out almost one hundred old slides for the family reunion. But when she was finished, she told me the sad truth: "You know, Dad," she said, "we don't have one slide of Nathan."

Now Nathan's older brother Jon would love that. He'd probably say Nathan was too ugly for a camera to take his picture anyway. But Jon's wrong. Nathan never shattered a lens; he never got in one. The fact is, the newness of that camera—like the newness of being an uncle—wore off.

Here's another sad truth. When Andrea was born, that camera was like a necklace to me. We've got a hundred pictures of her—or more. Her little brother's lucky if he's on a couple dozen.

Does a drawerful of pictures of Andrea—and a few scattered shots of her little brother—mean that we love Andrea more than David? Of course not. Does it mean that Andrea was a stunner when she was a kid? No. Does it mean that now David's life is ruined, knowing, as he does, that his mug shows up less frequently in scrapbooks? My goodness, I hope not.

The Hebrew word for *firstborn* in this passage is really something—literally, it means "womb-opener." Okay, I know such images aren't for family consumption, but I want you to realize what God means. God wants the people to "consecrate" the "womb-openers," to give them to their Creator. God wants the first kid, the one who gets all our attention.

Now before you jump to savage conclusions—no, the Israelites didn't sacrifice babies. God wants our firstfruits alive, not dead. God wants the very firstfruits of what we do. Why? Because our attention, our *full* attention, is important to God. I snapped so many pictures of my daughter when she was born that we're lucky she wasn't blinded by the flash. But she was the first, see? We didn't focus on David as much—not because we don't love him, but because he wasn't the first.

The principle here is not that the first child of every family should become a preacher—that's not it at all. What the passage suggests is that God wants our attention first—before anything else; and in order to get that, God demands that we swear over our firstfruits.

We might put it this way—on that slide show of our lives, God wants to be up on the screen more than anything or anybody: more than volleyball, soccer, kids, Nintendo, prom dresses, boyfriends, girlfriends, work (for me, writing), shopping, hunting pheasants, or that cottage up north.

God wants to be number one.

....

Especially when we're young, Lord, we've got so much of a world to discover. Help us never to lose sight of the important things. Keep us close to you. Strengthen us to always give you our firstfruits.
Amen.

NEVER FORGET

···

Read Exodus 13:8-10

Some European cemeteries attract American tourists—not because these graveyards explain how Europeans lived, but because they show how lots of North Americans and other Allied soldiers died. We visited one just last summer. It wasn't terribly large—no bigger than a football field, in fact—a spacious, perfectly manicured lawn between two long fields of tongue-shaped graves, dozens of them commemorating bodies without names.

The dead there, in that little cemetery outside of Oosterbeke, are mostly English. They were the British First Airborne Division, dropped onto Dutch soil almost fifty years ago for a battle that was meant to bring the Second World War to a quick and merciful end.

It was raining when we visited that little cemetery, but the downpour didn't dampen the enthusiasm of maybe forty or fifty "tommies," British vets, who were also visiting, decked out in wartime gear for a parade march to the memorial on the far end of the cemetery. They'd driven up in buses with their wives.

We watched them as the rain got heavier. Those old men formed a line and marched—some on canes, some on four-pronged walkers— all the way to the end of the field. Average age?—maybe 75. They weren't about to forget.

Almost fifty years ago, a Mrs. Knap, right there in Oosterbeke, told her kids to look up in the sky, where English troops were falling gracefully in billowing parachutes—thousands of them, like confetti in the wide sky, the promise of deliverance. To Mrs. Knap it meant the end of the Nazi occupation. All over town, people stood on roofs to cheer.

"Kids," Mrs. Knap said, pointing at the sky, "always remember this day because our friends are coming to chase our enemies away."

It didn't happen. The Brit paratroopers couldn't get to their objective, and the Allies' daring attempt to slash through the Nazi-held countryside failed. Of the 10,000 "tommie" paratroopers, only 2,200 returned. Nazi forces withstood an Allied attempt to capture a bridge over the Lower Rhine. Thousands of troops, on both sides, died.

Trying to stay out of the rain, we stood with some of the wives of the Brits, and when I remarked how incredibly neat the cemetery looked, one of them told me something I've not forgotten. She said each year schoolchildren in Oosterbeke are assigned a grave to decorate. Oosterbeke does not want to let its children forget the tommies that fell from the sky, only to die in an attempt to free their village.

Several times the exodus story we've just finished stresses the very same idea—telling the children, helping them remember. At Passover, many Jewish families pass on the story yet today, as if it had happened only last year.

My religion is not Jewish. I am a Christian. But the Passover celebration does not belong to Jews alone. It belongs to the people of God. In my family, we do not celebrate a Passover meal. We do not eat unleavened bread or bitter herbs. But we do partake of the body and blood of Christ Jesus, who came to save us—whose own blood, splashed on our lives, means that we too can be passed over, we too can be saved.

The exodus story, you see, belongs to all the people of God.

So don't forget it. Tell the children. Pass it on.

....

Lord, when we forget the story you've given us in your Word, we forget you. When we forget you, we forget your promises. Help us remember how you've loved generations of believers. Thank you for loving us. Thank you for sending your Son.
In his name, Amen.

THE DESERT FOX

....

Read Exodus 13:17-22; 14:1-4

Anthropomorphically. That's the word I'm thinking of today. If you can't pronounce it, don't worry; few of us can. What it means, as you may know, is "picturing God as if he were human." God is *not* human, but the Bible anthropomorphizes him in today's passage: it paints God Almighty in battle fatigues, the supreme "desert fox," the greatest military general ever to lead troops over the sands.

Tell you what, let's add to the picture. As long as the Bible starts it, let's fill in some details.

There God stands, hands down, leaning over a table. A shaded bulb swings just slightly from its cord, its cone of light shifting almost methodically across a gigantic map sprawled over the table top. God's got a wooden pointer in his hand, and he wears tin-rimmed glasses.

It's late at night, and the shuffle of marching feet goes on endlessly behind him. He brings the pointer down to the map, then raises it again, as if he changed his mind. He folds his arms, never taking his eyes off the table top.

The Desert Fox slaps the pointer off his open hand and raps the table twice. "This way," he says, even though there seems to be no one in the room. He points again at the map, and his lieutenants gather around him, as if appearing out of thin air.

"I'm worried about my people," God says. "If they face war, they might just turn around."

So he draws up a plan to avoid the obvious road through Philistine country because he knows the Egyptians are dug in there like desert badgers in thick sand fortifications. "We're going here," he says, and he points to the desert road up toward the Red Sea.

Those angelic lieutenants stir around on their military stools. Michael casts a glance at Raphael, who takes off his hat and wipes a line of sweat from his forehead. "The Red Sea?" Michael says.

God raps the map again with his pointer. "They've got to know," he says. "They have to know who's in charge here. We'll go by sea."

Raphael runs his hat band through his fingers. "We'll get to the sea, sir," he says, "and then what? You've got thousands of people down there, thousands—really."

"Pharaoh will think they're mixed up," the Lord says. He looks up almost causally. "Pharaoh will get his reports and chuckle. He will. He'll figure, 'That rebel bunch couldn't steer it's way out of an open grocery bag—let's take it to them."

"Sir," Raphael says, "it *is* the sea. We've got thousands down there and we'd have to go all the way to the Nile for a rubber raft."

God Almighty looks up from the table. He slaps the pointer off his hand once again, then lays it down. He straightens himself up and grabs the light, holding it straight.

"He'll send his men," he says to Raphael, as if he hadn't heard the question. "He'll send his chariots down and, believe me, nobody will come back who doesn't know for sure that this God they've been fighting is going to get the glory." He looks at his men and smiles. "The Egyptians will know that I am the Lord."

The Master of strategy, who never breaks a promise.

....

Dear Lord, we thank you for your faithfulness. We thank you that you've been with your people for generations, and that you will be with us too, in war and peace, in sunshine and storm. We thank you for your promise of a Savior, Jesus Christ. Amen.

THE PRICE OF FREEDOM

....

Read Exodus 14:5-14

"Sometimes you just get fed up," Shanna thought. "You get so fed up that you don't want to put up with it anymore. After all, America's a free country, isn't it?"

She was up in her room, mad as a hot wasp. She whipped out her jeans, grabbed a couple of T-shirts, then deliberately left everything open. For good measure she emptied her drawers all over the floor where her mother would find them and just scream.

She jammed her clothes in her old Budweiser duffle and stuck in an extra pair of shoes—high tops. She told herself the sky wasn't falling. Just because she'd been out late—big deal. Most of her friends didn't have to put up with the hassles she did, and she wasn't going to take it anymore. She'd spent her whole life as a slave!

Shanna was sick and tired of her parents' nitpicking: "Be in on time," they said. "Don't hang around with Bruce. Go to church. Make your bed. Study. Stay away from Durward's place. Don't do drugs." On and on, like some preachy cassette player you can't unplug. They were driving her crazy.

"I'm leaving," she told herself. "I'm walking downstairs and marching right through the living room. I'm not giving Ma the time of day. I've had it here. This place is a morgue and a dungeon and sweatshop, and I'm never coming back."

....

The cold seeped in through the windows of the old station wagon, even though they were closed. They were parked somewhere in Nebraska, Shanna thought, or maybe Colorado, at least a thousand miles away from home. The guy she was with seemed nice enough, but here they were in some rest stop, sleeping—he in the front seat, she in the back.

She wasn't sleeping either. She was too scared to sleep. He had a gun beneath the seat. He said he kept it because where he lived people lived or died by guns. She didn't find that very reassuring.

Shanna knew that at home her bed would be made, her room tidy and inviting. If she knew her mother, all her stuffed animals would be lined up straight as a pin, like always. And Mom would be crying, of course.

It would be warm, she thought longingly. And she wouldn't have a man in the front seat that she didn't even know, a man with a gun. Her room would be so warm . . .

....

Okay, it wasn't nice of the Israelites to scream at Moses in today's passage, but it was understandable. Even though they'd seen ten awful plagues, even though everything Moses had said had turned out perfectly true, they still complained. But chances are, so would we.

Freedom isn't as eternally rosy as some think. The Israelites wanted out of slavery. But once they were on their own, freedom looked downright dangerous—so dangerous, in fact, that the old slavery looked better.

Shanna is free, isn't she? But she's scared stiff, and you can't blame her. Freedom's often scary.

When the Iron Curtain's violent crash was heard around the world, millions scrambled for freedom, thinking that freedom was somehow salvation. But it isn't. Freedom isn't security. Freedom isn't even always very nice. Freedom takes guts and work. It's a great political idea, but it's never saved a soul.

Freedom, we know—great as it is—isn't really anything at all like salvation. Salvation belongs to the Lord.

....

Thank you for the freedoms that we have, Lord—
thank you for allowing us a political system that
grants us opportunity to say and think and worship
as we feel right. But help us also to understand
freedom's price—and the fact that we owe our
worship to you, not to an idea.
In Jesus' name, Amen.

MIRIAM'S STORY VII

....

Read Exodus 14:15-31

Of the line of chariots there seemed to be no end. We stood on the bluff at the edge of the water, and as far as we could see behind us, the dust rose, as if a legion of chariots were preparing to swallow every Hebrew in a cloud of death.

Thousands of us stood there, our cries reaching up to heaven. But no one seemed to answer. My brother himself, the prophet, stood at the water's edge, his eyes closed—as if he could, by his own will, save us.

My friend Elkinah hid her hands in the long sleeves of her robe to keep the ends from snapping in a wind so strong and full of sand that we had to lean to stay upright, our faces almost hidden. Both of us saw clearly, even though our eyes were full of fear. Hordes of Egyptian chariots in a cloud of sand—and in front of us nothing but the sea.

"Miriam," Elkinah said, "so tell me—is this God someone evil?"

"That is something no one should say," I told her.

In the strong and scouring wind, we nearly had to shout at each other.

She took my arms in her hands. "I had faith this God of Moses would

hold us safe in mighty hands, just as Moses said, that somewhere there would be for us a land of milk and honey."

We are old women—Elkinah and I. What kind of place is the wilderness for old women? That's what I asked myself. But that's not what I said.

"So you've quit on the Lord—is that it?" I said. "That's what you're saying now? You don't believe in God?"

Elkinah's hands fell quickly, and she swept her hood up and over her face as if she wouldn't talk to me.

"After all God has done?" I kept after her. "Elkinah, don't turn your face from me. Listen!" I stood where she couldn't see the chariots, but she turned her face. "Am I right?—after everything you have seen, you can still turn your back on the Lord? Is that what you're saying?"

She tried to walk away. She turned to the sea, but I kept after her because I wouldn't let her do what I feared I was already doing in my heart—forsaking our God.

"Shame, Elkinah," I screamed, but I was afraid, too—and I doubted the Lord. I had seen my brother's eyes, how they burned with God's vision, but there we stood at the edge of the sea, nothing behind us but Pharaoh's chariots of war. What were we to think?

And that's when I fell into Elkinah's arms. I was so tired. I couldn't say what I wanted to say anymore because I didn't believe it myself. You understand? I didn't trust the Lord to rescue us. No one did.

The wind screamed, but my friend Elkinah took me in her arms. "Miriam," she said. Her voice sounded different. "Miriam, look." She took my shoulders in her hands and turned me around to see a sight I never will forget. As I stood there in tears, with my own eyes I watched the waters part—I saw the hand of God open the sea for my people. God made a path for us. God made a way for us to walk to freedom.

I saw it. With these eyes, I watched it happen. And it's something I won't ever forget.

....

We can never thank you enough for our deliverance,
Lord, for saving us when we were unable to save
ourselves. Amen.

MIRIAM'S STORY VIII

....

Read Exodus 15:1-21 (after reading meditation)

We were old women. Long ago our strength had left our bodies. But once the waters parted, Elkinah and I—just like the rest—ran through the dry sea bed. God had done a miracle, but the desert was still overrun with Egyptian chariots. So we ran.

It seems now that we ran that whole distance. Maybe it was fear, maybe it was joy, and maybe a little of both. This God I'd given up on had once again saved us from death itself, put us safely down on dry land. Maybe we ran with God's strength.

I don't remember how long or how far that trip between walls of water was—only that once we were all across, the chariots had already begun to follow this miracle path through the sea. What God had done for us seemed once again to be too little—can you believe it? They were behind us, after all.

I don't have to tell you what happened. You know, don't you? You have heard the story so often that I don't have to go on.

And yet I must. You must never forget.

We stood up on the bank, the chariots now so close that the glints of their armaments seemed almost like the sparkles of a sea of death behind us. Elkinah and I, we stood on the banks, and watched my brother, the little boy I had taken home to my mother's arms. He raised his hand, and just like that the banks of the waters filled the channel of dry land.

I saw hundreds die. One after another the Egyptian chariots disappeared into the sea.

But we were safe. We were free. And what I shall never forget— and what you should never forget either—is that every time we were close to death, the God of our people, the God who has chosen us, also saved us. Every time I doubted, God was there. Every time death stampeded toward us, God picked us up as gently as a mother would and held us lovingly.

So I danced that night, my children. Elkinah and I and all the women—even the oldest ones—we danced as if the greatest battle of

all time had been won forever. I never once felt pain in these old bones. I never felt stiffness, and not once did I even say to myself that all of this celebration was too much. I danced for joy. I could have died that day for happiness.

And this is my song. Will you think of it now—remember it with me even though you weren't there? We will sing it the way we did then. Come, we'll dance around this table. We will praise God for our deliverance, for God has set us free.

Blessed be God's name! (Read Exodus 15:1-21)

....

Blessed be your name, Lord, for you will reign forever and ever. Amen.